Teaching Clarity,
Purpose and Motivation

Teaching Clarity, Purpose and Motivation

A Secondary School Adviser's Handbook

Dan Morrissey

AVOCUS
PUBLISHING

Inquiries should be directed to:
Avocus Publishing
P.O. Box 89
Gilsum, NH 03448

Editor: Alessandra Bianchi
Designer: Michel Newkirk

Printed and bound in the United States of America
First Edition

ISBN: 978-1-890765-07-1

CONTENTS

CHAPTER 3

SPRING FORWARD: Exercises, Assignments, and Worksheets for the Spring Semester

CHAPTER 4

Goal Setting Exercises   153

CHAPTER 5

Effectively Communicating with Advisee Parents   165

Further Reading/Resources   182

Why I Wrote This Book

A confluence of several separate, but memorable events put me on the path to writing this workbook. Many years ago, when I was new to teaching and even newer to advising, the Dean of Students canceled one of the school's "Assembly" periods so that advisers could spend some time with their advisees. There was no prescribed conversation prompt and no subject matter to discuss. Advisers were simply told to be present during the Assembly period in the location where they normally met with their advisees. The instructions assumed that advisers normally met with their advisees.

I was present. I bought doughnuts and juice and waited for my advisees to arrive. They arrived. They ate the doughnuts and drank the juice. They sat and stared at me, and I at them. The bell rang. They departed.

A few months later, there was another canceled Assembly and again, advisers were instructed to meet with their advisees. Not wanting a repeat of the Doughnut Staring Contest, I thought back to my own experiences from high school and hastily wrote a set of questions that I called, "Good Kid." It was loosely based on an exercise that a priest from my high school had done with my freshman Religious Studies class in 1980. (I have included the updated version of that exercise in this book as "Father Pusateri's Be a Good Kid," on page 68.) The exercise sparked great questions and conversations, and I was quite proud of myself for creating such a wonderful exchange during our meeting…until the next one.

A few months later, and a few months after that, assemblies were canceled so that advisers might meet with our advisees. At each meeting I would roll out the doughnuts, the juice, and my "Good Kid" exercise with great pride and satisfaction. Fairly quickly, the ensuing conversations became dull and hackneyed. I needed a new trick.

Around this time, I happened to pick up a copy of *Being Adolescent: Conflict and Growth in the Teenage Years*, by Mihaly Csikszentmihaly and Reed Larson. The book discusses the development of "life themes" and lays out the seeds of a positive psychological condition for which the authors later became famous, called "Flow." I began to ask myself, How

> *"What is learned in high school, or for that matter anywhere at all, depends far less on what is taught than on what one actually experiences in the place."*
> —E.Z. Friedenberg

could I help teenagers develop life themes or discover Flow? I hadn't a clue. Then one of my advisees, a smart, athletic, and popular student, shared with me one of her English papers that flip-flopped our relative positions of teacher and pupil.

In her paper, the student wrote of the hours she spent practicing her sport. When she practiced, she became better skilled and was able to translate all the moves she had mastered in drills and exercises into game situations. However, in other, non-athletic pursuits she felt unpracticed, nervous, and lacking in confidence.

She wrote: "I say bulls—to everyone who says practice makes perfect. Practice builds confidence, NOT perfection." The "aha moment" had arrived. I could not help students create life themes or find Flow; I could only help them build the confidence to do so through practice.

I searched the literature to find practices for developing confidence in teens. I came to know what I already knew: that there are no easy solutions or "How To" manuals. Instead there is a hint here, a strategy there, a suggestion buried beneath complex research in another source. From reading that student's paper, and the research that followed, sprang a whole series of goal-setting exercises, questions, and writing prompts aimed at helping teens identify, clarify, and refine their own goals. This book is a collection of those exercises to this point. I hope that there are more someday. I have tried to write the book in a simple, easy-to-follow manner so that anyone working with teenagers can pick it up and immediately put it to use.

Words cannot express my gratitude for and appreciation of my dear family, Erin, Declan, Owen and Mairead, for giving me the hours to research and write this handbook and for reading and listening to edit after edit. My family has also been my rock-solid, unwavering foundation as I worked to support my advisees. Thank you. Special thanks go to Gordon Coole, my teacher, mentor, friend, colleague, and confidante who, in the spring of 1988, called me and suggested I look into a positions at Phillips Andover Academy. Without that call, I would have never have stumbled into this challenging and rewarding world of independent schools. Nor would I likely have had the opportunity to spend a cumulative 20 years at Phillips Exeter Academy, where I have been honing and using these exercises with talented students, faculty, and administrators. A thank you also goes to Sharon Wang, who in 2004 said to me, "You should put what you do with your advisees into a book," thus planting the seed for this project. Finally, thank you to Alessandra Bianchi, Judith Peter, and the late Ernest Peter at Avocus Publishing, who believed in the project from the moment they read my submission.

I will end my note by saying, "Thank you" to readers and users of this handbook, something you might not ever hear from your most conscientious students or advisees. Thank you for using this book to help students find their own paths and identify the steps to stay on those paths.

– January 2012

Rationale for an Advising Curriculum

Adolescence is not a fatal disease; instead it is a time of great confusion when young minds become muddled with questions and thoughts that are self-doubting and self-defeating. My friend and colleague, psychiatrist Dr. Chris Thurber, describes teens as "neurologically impaired," since their pre-frontal lobes are still so underdeveloped that they struggle to make rational choices. Another friend, Patrice Baker, once told me, "Being a teenager is like being on an emotional roller coaster. You don't have to get on with them." If schools are the proverbial amusement parks where teens take their wild rides, advisers are the appointed chaperones who help encourage, support and guide them along the way.

In theory, this job involves the loftiest of goals. Advisers are charged with tracking a group of students' academic, social, and emotional progress as they advance through school. Much like parents, they specialize in helping students develop life skills, an overarching term encompassing such ennobling character traits as perseverance, resilience, empathy, trustworthiness, confidence, compromise, and humility. Advisers accomplish this by modeling the good behavior, as well as by listening, observing, knowing, and appreciating the unique natures of each of their charges. As Boston educator Peter Gow writes in his thoughtful book, *The Intentional Teacher*, "[T]he key to successful advising is simply having a keen interest in and awareness of each child and his or her environment, needs, and challenges."[1] Working in partnership with parents and other adults on campus who play an important role in the student's life, an adviser helps an advisee make the transition from adolescence to young adulthood.

That's the theory anyway. In practice, the process, however well-intentioned, is far from celestial. I often tell faculty new to Exeter that good advising is like making sausage: it can be an ugly, messy process, but the end results are to be savored! When I see good advising, it looks like what I call "objective parenting," or raising children by not linking our emotions to the peaks and valleys that come with child and teen development. As with the great amusement parks, the experience on the proverbial sidelines of adolescence can be nearly exciting as the rides. Both can churn your stomach or take your breath away.

Exeter's Adviser Handbook reminds readers that the term "adviser" comes from the French root of the word *viser*, meaning "to look forward with an aim," but this only scratches the surface of an adviser's job description. Good advisers wear many hats, including that of counselor, communicator, academic coach, disciplinarian, crisis manager, advocate, and mentor—not to mention pizza provider, sounding board, and voice of reason. (And let's not forget, in most cases they accomplish all of this while teaching a full course load and raising families of their own!) Advisers are there when students succeed, but are more often there when students fail. Good advisers actually allow students to fail, a rarity in 21st-century parenting. Advisers work with advisees to develop grit (a favorite new buzzword) and resiliency. They accomplish all of this, as Durango Institute Director Carol Hotchkiss writes, by "allowing teenagers to be teenagers."[2]

Adding to the challenge of this good work is the parent factor. Advisers, who act *in loco parentis* for their students while on campus, of course need to know how to handle actual parents. Allowing parents to be parents, particularly "fast track" parents at independent high schools, often requires deep reserves of diplomacy, empathy, and resolve. Rightly or wrongly, many of these parents see our schools as "grade factories" and the Yellow Brick Road to entrance into prestigious colleges. These parents have set very lofty, sometimes unattainable, goals for their sons and daughters. Psychologist A.A. Brooks identifies some of the potentially perilous consequences of such an approach[3] but my own technical term for the situation is the "Doris Effect," something to which good advising systems and good advisers never want to fall victim.

"Doris" is the name my own children gave to our satellite navigation system in the family van because they think that the electronic voice sounds like it would belong to someone of that name. Think about your own experience as a teenager: were you ever driving or walking somewhere when you became lost or unsure of which route to take to your final destination? How did you manage? If you are like me, you referred to a map, or you stopped and asked directions. You had to stop and think, maybe even ask another human being where to turn. If your experiences were anything like mine, you probably had to backtrack on more than one occasion. Maybe you were late to your destination, or maybe you didn't show up at all! Today, all we need to do is type the final destination into a computer and it figures out the fastest route, diverting us around traffic if necessary, all the while estimating our time of arrival with frightening accuracy. If we do somehow take a wrong turn, we simply wait for the computer to re-calculate a new route. To push the metaphor, good advisers don't map the routes for their advisees; they help their advisees map their own routes.

Sounds simple, right? In my experience nothing at schools is more difficult. Students have expectations of their adviser; parents have expectations of their student's adviser; the institution has expectations for the adviser; at independent schools, the admissions office has advertised what the adviser's role is; and the advisers have expectations, as well. None of these expectations are in balance with one another and none take into account that we only have so much time and energy!

As fate would have it, the stakes for being a good advisor have never been higher. In our era of helicopter parenting, and 24/7 digital information saturation, families crave real, not virtual, solace. Research has documented that the next generation of students and parents will choose the school that they feel has the most *supportive* and *healthy* curriculum.[4,5,6] Families still want Johnny and Susie to go to Harvard, but they don't want them to have nervous breakdowns along the way.

The good news is that adviser programs have been a longstanding presence in independent boarding and day schools, and are increasingly becoming more common in public and charter schools. Typically, a faculty member is assigned between 10-12 students, and meets at regular frequencies (i.e. weekly, bi-weekly) to check in and track students' progress. Such programs may be called "mentoring programs," "homeroom," "family meeting," or "schoolhouse meeting," but most often are referred to as "advisee groups," or "advisory." Ideally, schools set aside meeting times for advisee groups and build them into the academic schedule. Common sense suggests that such routine faculty-student encounters are a good idea, and educational research data backs this up. For example, adviser-advisee programs have been linked to decreased drop-out rates in high schools by the Wisconsin Department of Public Instruction,[7] as well as improved grades by the Tolland, Connecticut school district.[8]

But supportive data and consensus about advising's importance only take you so far. You've got 10-12 teens in a room, now what? In my more than 20 years' experience, I have yet to find a bullet-proof secret of success to being a good adviser. Teachers who are popular with kids may or may not be effective advisers; the same can be said for frosty disciplinarians. What works with one group may fall flat with another. Conversations with my peers suggest I am not the only one enduring the Great Donut Staring Contest. Recently, in a survey of more than 200 faculty members at independent schools around the country, several common themes emerged. "We don't know what to do." Advisers suffer from a "lack of confidence when dealing with certain issues." They feel they need "more educational opportunities that will focus on problematic issues (i.e. preventative, intervention, and postvention [sic] techniques.").[9] When asked to define "postvention" this faculty member told me that she felt confident dealing with crises, but was less comfortable helping students ensure they didn't occur again.

My peers are no slouches, and their cries for help struck a chord. Despite widespread agreement on the utility and effectiveness of adviser programs, there are few resources or formal curriculums actually describing what the process entails. How do these programs really work? What can an adviser do to assist advisees as they progress through the school?

> "There is something in every one of you that waits and listens for the sound of the genuine in yourself. It is the only true guide you will ever have. And if you cannot hear it, you will all of your life spend your days on the ends of strings that somebody else pulls."
> –Howard Thurman

How does an adviser get to know his or her advisees during the meetings? How can an individual adviser positively impact each and every one of his or her advisees with limited time and resources available?

This handbook is designed to answer these questions. It contains a wide selection of exercises and writing assignments that I have collected, devised, and improvised over the past 20 years in my various capacities as adviser, faculty member, administrator, and Dean of Students. Amazingly, this track record corresponds to advising a student population numbering nearly 1,000. Yet as any parent of a teenager knows, just when you think you've got them figured out, they move the goal posts on you. Teens may not be the only ones on the roller coaster, after all!

How to Use This Workbook

The exercises in this book use an Organizational Behavior term known as "double loop learning." Double loop learning is practiced by calling time out, or stopping the action and reviewing what has happened up to that point. This review is done very carefully and two central questions are explored: "What worked?" and "What didn't?" The responses to these questions are evaluated and from them a path for the future is charted.[10] My hope is that this book will serve as a roadmap for the wild journey otherwise known as advising teens, but I encourage you to stop every once in awhile, check for directions, and make sure that you are still on the correct course.

The book is organized along the academic calendar, with progressive exercises beginning in the fall of the ninth grade year and moving through to the spring of the twelfth grade. Although the workbook is divided by grade, advisers can adjust and transfer exercises from any grade or section. I mention in the "Overview and Suggested Use" section of each exercise whether, in my experience, an exercise is better suited for a younger audience, or more mature group, or a group whose positive interpersonal dynamics have already developed.

Most of the exercises include discussion prompts and a rough estimate of how much time they will take. It is crucial for advisers to allow for discussion and debriefing of the exercises; some of the most valuable learning occurs when individual advisees share their thoughts with the group.

The worksheets are divided by the objectives they are intended to develop. Shown at right is an example with all the worksheet categories listed. Most exercises will have two or three of these areas, indicated in shaded tabs along the right hand edge of the page, as well as listed on the upper left hand side of the Overview/Suggested Use pages. The exercises are also identified by suggested appropriate grade levels, in shaded boxes in the upper corner of left hand pages.

Though the exercises vary, they are all designed to move advisers and advisees toward what I have become convinced is the most crucial step in teen self-actualization and self-motivation: goal setting.

9TH GRADE

Goal Setting

Character and Leadership Development

Values Clarification

Group Dynamics/ Social Development

Academic/Study Skills

Adjustment/Transition/ Role in School

Health/Life Skills

Sample above of suggested grade level and exercise objectives.

We'll review goals and goal setting in a moment, but first, an explanation of the assignments and discussion prompts in this handbook. Each chapter contains approximately five exercises per term for each grade level. The exercises are designed to get students to think about their academic, social, and emotional progress while at the same time allow them to connect and get to know one another better. They also help advisers become better acquainted with their advisees. Several assignments help advisers prompt advisees to refresh, evaluate, and reset their goals at the midterm and at the end of the term.

Ideally, advisers should hold advisee meetings once a week to every ten days if such times are not already built into their school's schedule. During these meetings, advisees should expect to complete an assignment and to have discussion on that assignment. Of course, schools that have scheduled adviser/advisee times or built-in meetings may prescribe certain administrative tasks during these times (filling out forms, schedules, surveys, etc.), but after a few weeks, students should be in the habit of completing a writing assignment when there is no prescribed topic or agenda for an advisee group meeting.

To assist in keeping track of where they are in the school year and possible meeting topics and agendas, I recommend that advisers keep an 'advisee' calendar. This is an idea that my friend and Exeter colleague, Carol Cahalane, shared with me. Carol creates a calendar each year to remind herself of important dates and time lines. It's a strategy she borrowed from a notoriously industrious person, Martha Stewart. In the first few pages of each issue of *Martha Stewart Living* magazine, the domestic diva shares with her readers her "to do" list for the month. An advisee calendar need not be more than a paper calendar with notes, meeting times, advisee birthdays, and important school dates notated, although some more technologically advanced advisers might create an "icalendar" that will update to an iPad or iPhone automatically.

When I create my advisee calendar each year (the pencil and paper kind, not the electronic), I add important dates during the school year such as midterms, finals, rivalry weekends, and long weekends. After nearly a quarter century as an adviser, I have a sizable history to draw from when planning out the school year. At Exeter, homework seems to go in cycles of about three weeks where the volume and intensity increases gradually and then decreases for a brief one or two day period before beginning to ramp up again. It seems that classroom teachers do some type of assessment—a paper, a lab report, a test, a project—every three weeks. I plot those cycles on my advisee calendar and I remind my advisees and their parents when I think the cycle is beginning. These mesocycles (small cycles within a larger one) are overlaid on a macrocycle (the larger cycle of an entire school year) of school life—dances, standardized tests, concerts, school plays, auditions, college applications, the "Big Game"—which, if the timing is right (or wrong!) can add more stress and more work to individual advisees' schedules. It is crucial to observe the rhythm of your particular school and if you are a newcomer, to seek the advice of more seasoned advisers and teachers. If you are an experienced teacher or adviser, it is crucial to share your knowledge and understanding of the rhythm of the school (and perhaps your advisee calendar) with less experienced teachers and advisers.

To get things moving, I like to open adviser meetings with some ice breakers: casual, thought-provoking questions that invite creative answers. In this spirit, I have included a quotation at the top of each worksheet page preceding each exercise. Sometimes just talking about the quote helps students get their minds centered, focused, and ready to participate in the exercise more fully. Another resource I like is a commercially available product called Chat Pack, which contains over 150 open-ended questions that are great conversation starters. The questions are age-appropriate and fun ("Of all the movie characters you have seen, which one do you believe is most like you?") and also help advisers get to know their advisees. Chat Packs are available at http://www.writersstore.com/chat-pack.

Advisers should keep an "advisee folder" for each advisee. The folder need not be extravagant or large—it can even be an envelope. Some advisers, especially those advising underclassmen, might want to have their advisees decorate or personalize the folders. At the very least, advisees should clearly mark the folder as their own.

Advisers should have ready at the beginning of each group meeting the advisee folders, paper, writing utensils, markers, etc., and the exercise for the day. At the end of the meeting, collect students' completed exercises and place in their folders. They will serve as handy references for both adviser and students as the year progresses.

Goal Setting: Some Context

As I stated earlier, I set out to "teach" self-esteem and quickly discovered that I was trying to nail down a moving target. Author Robert Evans says it best in his book, *Family Matters:* "Self-esteem is too often misunderstood as being produced by the outcome of an activity—whether the child wins the game—rather than the effort the child puts into it. But it is when we confront issues and respond to challenges, regardless of their outcome that we experience positive, self-affirming thoughts and feelings."[11] Teaching students to set goals, and to help them set steps by which they can achieve goals, is the greatest gift we can give to them.

There is no shortage of professional research demonstrating that the setting of goals is one of the most effective ways to assist teens as they wrestle with social pressure and complex tasks. The benefits are manifold. Goal setting assists teens in self-efficacy—that is, knowing what to do in order to accomplish a goal and then doing it.[12] Setting goals helps students achieve satisfaction and allows them to accurately and objectively appraise performance.[13] Author Thomas Ryan recognized this as far back as 1970 when he observed in his book, *Intentional Behavior,* "it seems a simple fact that human behavior is affected by conscious purposes, plans, intentions, tasks and the like." [14] More recently, study of the relationship between academic performance and setting personal goals has demonstrated that Ryan was correct. As Locke, Saari, Shawn, and Latham conclude in their article, *Goal Setting and Task Performance*: "The beneficial effect of goal setting is one of the most robust and replicable findings in the psychological literature" [15]

In 2010, Dominique Morisano led a group of researchers at McGill University who also found that goal setting plays a crucial role in academic achievement, creating a feedback loop between commitment and attainment. The loop becomes a cycle; as a student achieves a goal, he or she gains confidence and an understanding of what helped achieve the goal, and therefore the student sets new goals and the cycle repeats itself. These same authors point to a method by which the feedback loop is "kick started"; they say that a student must first "clarify the desired outcome," then specify "the path to the goal completion," and also "establish benchmarks by which progress can be evaluated." [16]

Martin Covington reports in *Goal Theory, Motivation, and School Achievement* that "adopting learning goals was positively associated with deep-level processing, persistence, and high effort, a combination that also led to increases in achievement." [17]

Middle school teacher Howard Johnson lists patterns of behaviors that "achievers" exhibit. Specifically, he writes that, "Achievers engage in anticipatory behavior, planning for tomorrow, next week, next summer or for the long-term future." [18]

Other authors use slightly different terms for goals and goal setting. Mihaly Csikszentmihaly and Reed Larson write about the importance of teens developing "life themes," in their ground-breaking study published in 1984, *Being Adolescent: Conflict and Growth in the Teenage Years*. They cite the following study of adult men:

> "[H]alf were successful intellectuals — professors, physicians, lawyers, and politicians—and the other half blue-collar workers. The childhood environment for all thirty was similar as it could be: Both groups came from poor immigrant families, both were equally plagued by illness, alcoholism, illiteracy, and poverty. Yet somehow half escaped its entropic [the author's term for disorder] background and achieved rare heights of complexity, while the other half led lives that were predictable given the conditions of their childhood. What made one group able to reshape its life conditions?
>
> There might have been many reasons that we have not begun to fathom. But one clear difference was that practically all the men who broke away from the constraints in which they were born had developed in adolescence goals that were to focus their energies for the rest of their lives. Each constructed for himself a *life theme*, a set of challenges that kept him struggling, and that forced him to develop skills of a rare complexity. The men whose lives were predictable did not create such a scheme." [19]

As advisers, we are in the perfect position to assist students in developing goals and life themes that are so important for success. Please note that I have been careful to use the terms "setting," "creating," and "developing" when discussing goals. Our responsibility is to help students develop their own goals and chart their individual courses by which they will achieve them, but students must achieve all of these milestones on their own.

It is clear from a large body of research that the setting of and subsequent work toward attaining goals is essential to helping adolescents focus their energy and time, and to giving them direction. As advisers proceed with this noble work, it is important to agree on a common definition for the term, "goal." I like the simple, useful explanation offered by Locke, Saari, Shaw, and Latham in *Goal Setting and Task Performance*: A goal is "what an individual is trying to accomplish; it is the object or aim of an action."[20]

On a related note, it is also useful to consider the distinction between what a goal *is*, versus what a goal *should* be. Goals are most helpful and effective when they are difficult and challenging. Goals that are easily achieved or achieved with little effort do not allow for proper feedback nor do they allow students to make future goals incrementally more challenging. An individual involved in business might say that goals that lack challenge are not 'scalable,' that is, they do not grow in complexity as the student moves through higher level courses and opportunities.

In order to be most effective, goals should share two basic characteristics. They should be specific; and they should be based on process, rather than achievement or results. Examples of unspecific, achievement- and results- based goal are to "score three goals a game," or "get a perfect score on the SAT." Examples of specific, process-based goals include, "I'm going to be the first person to get to practice every day, and I'm going to work on my shooting," or "I'm going to spend 20 minutes a day working in my SAT prep book." In other words, goals should be appropriately challenging, but also realistic and feasible.

Finally, goals should have a temporal element—a date or time at which they should be achieved or evaluated—and contain benchmarks by which their status can be measured.

Goals should be written down, in other words, so that a road map can be drawn from them. Timetables and signposts make this task easier.

1. Peter Gow, *The Intentional Teacher* (Gilsum: Avocus Publishing, 2009): 202.

2. Carol Hotchkiss and Edward Kowalchick, *Building a Residential Curriculum* (Durango: Durango Institute Press, 2002): 35.

3. A.A. Brooks, *The Perils Facing Children of Fast Track Parents* (Byefield: Independent School Health Association, 1997): 17.

4. B. Poirot and D. Richard, "Connecting with Kids: Boarding School rather than boarding School," *Healthy Schools, Healthy Choices*, ed. L. Crosier (Gilsum: Avocus Publishing, 1992): 15.

5. P. Kane, "Boarding Schools & Adolescence" speech presented at meeting of trustees, Miss Porter's School, Farmington, CT. (January 1997): 16.

6. D. Hicks, "The Strange Fate of the American Boarding School," *The American Scholar* (Autumn 1996): 534.

7. Wisconsin Department of Public Instruction – AYP Program literature http://dpi.wi.gov/ssos/ayp_handbook.html.

8. Tolland, CT School District Adviser Handbook http://www.csde.state.ct.us/public/der/ssp/SCH0607/sr119.pdf.

9. D. Morrissey, *Toward Assisting and Supporting Girls in a Boarding School Environment: A Handbook for Educators* (unpublished).

10. C. Argyris, *Organizational Learning II* (Reading: Addison-Wesley, 1996): 21-23.

11. R. Evans, *Family Matters: How Schools Can Cope with the Crisis in Childrearing* (San Francisco: Jossey Bass, 2004): 32.

12. M. Covington, "Goal Theory, Motivation, and School Achievement: An Integrative Review," *Annual Review of Psychology* (2000): 174.

13. E. Locke, K. Shaw, L. Saari, G. Latham, "Goal Setting and Task Performance," *Psychological Bulletin*, Vol. 90, No. 1 (1981): 126.

14. T. Ryan, *Intentional Behavior* (New York: Ronald Press, 1970): 18.

15. Locke *et al.*, 145.

16. D. Morisano, J. Hirsh,, J. Peterson, R. Pihl, B. Shore, "Setting, Elaborating, and Reflecting on Personal Goals Improves Academic Performance," *Journal of Applied Psychology*, Vol. 95, No. 2 (2010): 256.

17. M. Covington, "Goal Theory, Motivation, and School Achievement: An Integrative Review," *Annual Review of Psychology* (2000): 175.

18. H. Johnson, *"From Advisory Programs to Restructured Adult-Student Relationships: Restoring Purpose to the Guidance Function of the Middle School Level,"* (Reston: NASSP, March 1997): 3.

19. M. Csikszentmihalyi, R. Larson, *Being Adolescent, Conflict and Growth in the Teenage Years* (La Vergne: Basic Books, 1984): 279.

20. Locke *et al.*, 126.

CHAPTER 1

Setting the Stage, Advising Before Students Arrive on Campus

Getting to know new advisees is crucial for starting the school year with a level of comfort and preparedness for the academic, social, and emotional challenges that lie ahead. By reaching out to parents, advisers also establish a level of understanding and expectation that helps promote a healthy partnership between school and home.

It is also essential that advisers allow returning students to reintroduce themselves and to be updated on other advisees' activities over the summer months. High school is a time of unbelievable, rapid growth and development, and even a 10-week separation will result in changes advisers might not immediately see.

This chapter gives advisers ready-to-use templates for communicating with new and returning advisees and their parents during the summer months before the start of school. It also contains examples of effective adviser/parent communication. There's a checklist for advisers to follow while helping advisees (whether new or returning) smoothly transition to school. As with all exercises in this book, feel free to tweak and adjust some of the fine print to suit your particular school.

> *"The true delight is in the finding out, rather than in the knowing."*
> –Isaac Asimov

I (Want To) Know
What You Did This Summer!

Overview and Suggested Use:

Whether students are new to school or returning, it is helpful for advisers to know what their advisees did over the summer. This will allow the adviser to open conversations with advisees in the early weeks and months of school and to get to know the advisee group better. This questionnaire is designed to collect information on advisees' summer activities. Advisers can e-mail it or send it on paper, but it should be completed and returned before school begins.

Materials:

Email or paper copies, email addresses or home addresses, and self-addressed, stamped envelopes for all advisees.

I (Want to) Know What You Did This Summer!

What is the least academic or school-like thing you did this summer?

What was the most academic thing you did this summer?

What is your favorite song from the summer?

What was your favorite day this past summer?

- Where were you?

- What were you doing?

- Who were you with? (Were you alone?)

What world event most concerned you this summer?

What are your concerns or fears about school this year?

What are you most looking forward to at school?

Overview and Suggested Use:

New advisees can always benefit from learning strategies for success. The following is a sample note to new students. It is also a good idea to send this communication to parents of new advisees, so they can discuss its contents with their sons and daughters.

Materials:

E-mail or paper copies of the message, e-mail addresses or home addresses for all advisees.

Greetings, Advisees!

This is a long email and it contains a great deal of important information that will help you make a smooth transition to your life at your new school. It may be best to print it and read it several times.

Over the years, I have had the privilege of working with hundreds of talented and gifted students and faculty. I have heard many theories on how new students can make the most of their time at your new school. Below are some tips that I have collected over my two decades of independent-school teaching, coaching, dorm service, advising, and administration. I send them to you now so that you can practice these tactics prior to the start of school. Here are some strategies to consider:

Set Goals for Yourself:

Students enroll at your new school for many different reasons. Most students are seeking new opportunities, whether those opportunities center around academics, athletics, extracurricular activities, or social opportunities. What binds us all together at your new school is the pursuit of academic excellence. To put oneself on a course for academic excellence, one must set goals. Setting goals is a task that requires quiet reflection, so think about these questions:

- What do I want to get out of my experience at my new school?
- How might I go about achieving these things?
- What might get in the way of my success at school and how do I avoid these pitfalls?

I will be writing to you on this topic again soon, and in that note I will give you specific instructions on how to set goals for yourself. In the meantime, start thinking about your goals now!

Be Where You're Supposed to Be and Be on Time:

Your school's daily schedule is filled with classes, meetings, extracurricular activities, and study periods. It is our experience that many students need time to adjust to the academic schedule and pace of life.

Following are some simple strategies you can practice before school starts that will help you adjust more quickly and more efficiently to your school's schedule and routines.

Make regular sleep patterns a habit:

During the summer, keep or establish regular sleep patterns. Once at your new school, you should try to be in bed with lights out by 11 p.m. Classes usually begin at 8:00 a.m., and we expect all students to be prepared to participate in class discussions. I encourage you to start practicing this sleeping schedule as soon as you can.

Develop a bedtime ritual:

Some teens need a bedtime ritual to settle themselves down before they can sleep. Work to develop a ritual if you have a hard time falling asleep. Effective rituals include light reading, listening to slow, quiet music, or taking a quick shower. These rituals should be completed by 11 p.m.

"The more I see, the more I see there is to see."
–John Sebastian

Use an alarm clock:

High school-aged students are masters at sleeping through alarm clocks or pushing the "snooze button" too many times. Purchase a good alarm clock and learn how to set it; practice waking up to it by placing it in different areas of the room. My experience has been that students wake more easily if they need to get out of bed to turn off an alarm. Another location strategy is to place something over the clock (like a milk crate) that must be moved to turn the alarm off.

The type of clock used is also important. Stereo alarm clocks or alarm clocks that use music are less likely to work. Most students need something more heavy-duty. Alarm clocks that your new school students have used with success are the vibrating and the gradual light varieties. Check out www.hammacher.com or www.harriscomm.com.

During the summer, do not have your parents wake you up—learn to be awakened by the sound of your own alarm.

Wear a watch:

Sounds too simple to be true, but it works! Often, the first question asked by a student who is regularly late is, "What time is it?"

Many students use cell phones to keep time or rely on friends to tell them the time. At your new school, neither of these strategies works. All students need to wear a watch!

Avoid caffeine or other stimulants, especially before bedtime:

Prior to bedtime, limit the consumption of food and drinks containing caffeine. Read the nutritional information labels on what you eat or drink during those hours.

Avoid naps:

Students who take long naps during their free time disrupt their sleep/wake cycles. If you must take a nap, keep it to about 20 minutes.

Students new to a boarding school should use the "buddy system":

Find an experienced boarding student who is willing (there are many!) to wake you up in the morning for the first month of school. Many students employ this system throughout their school career to be sure they do not miss important, early-morning appointments.

Students new to a boarding school should avoid long-distance "wake-up calls":

It is our experience that parental wake-up calls, although well-intentioned, actually do a disservice to students as they strive to learn independence and life skills.

Be Prepared:

Students who take an organized approach to their studies are more likely to enjoy academic success.

Some simple, general tips to help you in your daily preparation:

- Make sure that studying is done in a quiet room or area that is free of distractions.
- Make sure that work is done during a scheduled time and keep that scheduled time sacrosanct.
- Create a file system. Divide a box large enough to hold file folders upright into sections—one for each subject you'll take. As you complete chapters or units, you'll have a handy place to put all of your notes, handouts, quizzes, and tests organized by subject. You will save yourself a great deal of time before exams by already having your material organized.
- Make sure your study area is neat and has enough room for spreading out work.
- Make sure that assignments are carefully recorded in an assignment book (many schools provide this for you upon your arrival; it doesn't hurt to check).

Use a calendar:

Buy a daily planner for yourself or register for an online calendar and start putting *any* dates, meetings, or appointments in it. Refer to it regularly. Put doctors' appointments, birthdays, and anything else into the book so that you get into the habit of recording items and looking at the appointment book regularly.

Learn how to set reminders for important deadlines:

Work this summer on developing a system that works for **you** to remind yourself of impending deadlines. Useful possibilities include post-it notes, cell phone reminders, or an assignment book. Over the years, we have observed that parents calling and emailing reminders from home is not the most effective method to help students stick to deadlines.

Check your phone, email messages, and the school bulletin boards daily:

Your new school uses email, voicemail, regular mail, and bulletin boards to communicate important messages to students. Check these every day!

Use Free Time Wisely:

Free periods, downtime, and "hangin' out":

Most likely, you will have open, unscheduled periods of time built into your calendar. Successful students use their free time to organize work, look ahead to upcoming assignments, create task lists, and divide tasks among available blocks of time.

...many students need time to adjust to the academic schedule and pace of life.

Everything in moderation:

Use videogames, video chat, IM, Facebook, online movies, and screen time wisely. We all need downtime—sometimes it is healthy to simply be entertained, but monitor screen time wisely and set limits for yourself!

Stay Healthy:

Make good choices in the dining halls:

Eat breakfast every day.

Prior to attending your new school, travel to a cafeteria-style restaurant like Luby's, Picadilly's, or Golden Corral and survey all of the choices before making a selection. Choose portions that are appropriate. Students at your new school share the dining halls/cafeteria and eat with faculty and staff; however, students make their own food selections.

Get regular, vigorous exercise:

The beneficial effects of regular, vigorous exercise on both body and spirit have been well-documented. Built into your new school schedule are opportunities for you to get regular exercise, whether it's on an interscholastic team or within the Physical Education program. You should come to campus with good, supportive footwear and exercise clothes.

It is best to arrive at your new school with good exercise habits in place. Work this summer to get daily, vigorous, aerobic exercise to help maintain your stamina and energy levels.

Take steps to avoid illness:

The most effective ways to prevent the flu and other droplet-borne diseases are to:

- Wash your hands after every contact and before you eat.
- If you cannot get to a sink, use a waterless hand cleaner.
- Carry Kleenex in your pocket or backpack and use it.
- Drink plenty of fluids, especially (non-caffeinated) water.
- Eat high-vitamin foods such as fruits, vegetables, and grains.
- Get outside and do some physical activity.
- Open your window to air out your room once a day.
- Carve out quality sleep time to avoid an overtired immune system.
- Boarders should practice good housekeeping in your room. (Washing off doorknobs, keyboards, phones, faucets, and other high-contact surfaces.)
- Let your roommate (boarders), friends, and adviser know when you are feeling sick.
- Boarders should add moisture to your room at night with a humidifier (if allowed) or a pan of water by your bedside.
- Get plenty of sleep (but do not nap for long periods during the day)
- Replace your toothbrush often.

Maintain Balance and a Positive Attitude:

Take time away from campus:

This is important. Simply walking around the grounds of your new school for a change of scenery can be re-energizing.

Keep up your favorite hobbies and routines:

Keep doing the things that you enjoy doing. Stay in touch with those activities that bring you pleasure, whether it be physical activity, music, leisure reading, painting, etc. Try to make time for yourself.

Trust yourself:

There will be a lot of new influences, ideas, personalities, pressures, expectations, distractions, attractions, and stimuli. It will be both exciting and challenging. Trying to figure out where you belong in this environment can, at first, be difficult; expect that, work with trusted adults in the your school community, and trust yourself.

Never Be Afraid to Ask a Question and Be Proactive in Seeking Help!

You have an adviser specifically to help you with this. You have entered an environment where there are many new people and new things to do, along with many new responsibilities and rules. It is important that you get out, meet people, and try new things. There is no way that any one student can know everything and do everything for him- or herself. Ask for help when you need it!

End-of-Summer Goal Setting

Goal Setting

Academic/Study Skills

Overview and Suggested Use:

As summer turns to fall, it is crucial for advisers to lay the groundwork with advisees to help them develop goals for themselves for the upcoming school year. For advisees who are returning to school, advisers can help remind them what their goals were for the previous year. For new students, advisers can help them reflect prior to their arrival on campus on what they are looking to gain from their academic and social experiences.

Materials:

Email or paper copies, email or home addresses for all advisees, who should be sent the following letter:

For Returning Advisees:

I have returned the goals you wrote out before leaving for summer break. You might remember that I asked you to write down three goals, the first being a goal for this term, the second a goal for the year, and lastly a goal for after graduation. Those goals are enclosed.

Please re-read the goals you set for yourself. Then:

- Go to a quiet, comfortable place and spend some time (10-15 minutes) evaluating whether or not you reached your goals.

- Write yourself or a friend (adult or otherwise) a letter that clearly states either how you were able to reach your goals, or what prevented you from doing so. Don't worry, you aren't going to send the note to anyone; it just helps to have someone in mind when writing.

Be Specific.

Be specific about each goal and specific about what you did or did not do so that your goals were reached or not reached.

Write out new goals. Select goals that you would like to achieve for the term, the year, and by graduation. Avoid achievement-oriented benchmarks like, "My goal is to get straight A's!" or "I want to make the varsity team." Instead set processed-based goals such as, "My goal is to study for two hours a night without interruption," "My goal is to go to extra help sessions three times a week," or "My goal is to be the first at practice each day and the last person to leave the field every day." Write down your goals; again, please be specific. Place them in an envelope, sign it, and send it to me before school begins.

For New Advisees:

In my previous note, I mentioned that it is important to have a set of goals to work toward at school. It has been my experience that students who identify a set of specific goals approach their studies in a more serious, organized manner, and are better able to manage setbacks should they occur.

It would be good for you to set a few goals for yourself for the first term. The following exercise should help.

- Go to a quiet, comfortable place and spend some time (10-15 minutes) thinking about the upcoming school year.

- Pretend that you are at home during the school's first break or vacation. Imagine that you are sitting in your room. Write a letter to yourself or a friend (adult or a peer) about the first few months of school. How were your first few months at school? What were your study skills like? Did you manage your time well? Did you work as hard as you could on your academics? Don't worry, you aren't going to send the note to anyone; it just helps to have someone in mind when writing.

- Write out goals. Select goals that you would like to achieve by that first break. Avoid achievement-oriented benchmarks like, "My goal is to get straight A's!" or "I want to make the varsity team." Instead set process-based goals like, "My goal to study for two hours a night without interruption," "My goal is to go to extra help sessions three times a week," or "My goal is to be the first at practice each day and the last person to leave the field every day." Write down the goals; again, be specific. Place them in an envelope, sign it, and send it to me before school begins.

Adviser Checklist for New Students

Overview and Suggested Use:

The first four to six weeks is a crucial time for new students to acclimate and assimilate into a new school. There are some simple steps that advisers can take to help ease a new advisee's transition. The following checklists, one for new day students and one for new boarding students, help advisers walk advisees through the challenges of the first several weeks of school. The lists can be tailored to fit the needs of any school.

Materials:

Paper copies of the list below, with additions or deletions based on the policies, practices, and culture of your school.

Adviser Checklist/Checkpoints

New Boarding Students

Name: _____

WEEK ONE:

- ☐ Room key operational
- ☐ Mailbox combination works
- ☐ Dorm phone working (voice mail is set-up)

Review:

- ☐ Always lock door and take the key
- ☐ Large sums of cash should be deposited with bank/school bank.
- ☐ Passports, I-20, F-1 stored in the Dean's Office safe (International Students only)
- ☐ Internet in room operational
- ☐ E-mail account operational (Reminded to check daily)
- ☐ Able to print to a printer
- ☐ Able to save a document to the network
- ☐ Daily schedule worked out
- ☐ Adviser emergency contact posted/programmed
- ☐ Dorm Head emergency contact posted/programmed
- ☐ Dorm emergency contact posted/programmed
- ☐ Permission levels reviewed
- ☐ Check that appropriate meds are in infirmary/health center, not in room
- ☐ Has a "meal buddy" or group
- ☐ Been to one on-campus Student Activities event
- ☐ Been to one on-campus athletic/drama/music/dance/art event
- ☐ Been to one off-campus (chaperoned) Student Activities event
- ☐ Attended sport or PE
- ☐ Has on-campus plans for upcoming weekend

WEEK TWO:

- ☐ Roommate (if applicable) conversation
- ☐ Contact made with parents
- ☐ Adviser emergency contact communicated
- ☐ Dorm Head emergency contact communicated
- ☐ Dorm emergency contact communicated
- ☐ Out of Town process reviewed
- ☐ Been to second on-campus Student Activities event
- ☐ Been to second on-campus athletic/drama/music/dance/art event
- ☐ Been to second off-campus (chaperoned) Student Activities event
- ☐ Knows the mall bus schedule and procedure(s)
- ☐ Has on-campus plans for upcoming weekend
- ☐ Attended "club sign up" and signed up for at least one club

WEEK THREE:

- ☐ Has been contacted by club head and plans on attending one meeting (knows location of meeting)

WEEK FOUR/FIVE:

- ☐ Midterms reviewed/discussed with student
- ☐ Midterms reviewed/discussed with parents
- ☐ Respond to any academic red flags
- ☐ Communicate above (dorm head/DOS/parents)
- ☐ Document above
- ☐ Preview fall term breaks/travel policies with students and parents

Adviser Checklist/Checkpoints

New Day Students

Name: _____

WEEK ONE:

☐ Locker combination works

☐ Knows the bus schedule and procedure(s)

Review:

☐ Always lock locker and take the key

☐ E-mail account operational (Reminded to check daily)

☐ Able to print to a printer

☐ Able to save a document to the network

☐ Daily schedule worked out

☐ Adviser emergency contact posted/programmed

☐ Emergency contact posted/programmed

☐ Permission levels reviewed

☐ Check that appropriate meds are with the nurse

☐ Has a "meal buddy" or group

☐ Been to one on-campus Student Activities event

☐ Been to one on-campus athletic/drama/music/dance/art event

☐ Been to one off-campus (chaperoned) Student Activities event

☐ Attended sport or PE

☐ Has plans with new schoolmates for upcoming weekend

WEEK TWO:

☐ Contact made with parents

☐ Adviser emergency contact communicated

☐ School emergency contact communicated

☐ Been to second on-campus Student Activities event

☐ Been to second on-campus athletic/drama/music/dance/art event

☐ Been to second off-campus (chaperoned) Student Activities event

☐ Has on campus plans for upcoming weekend

☐ Attended "club sign up" and signed up for at least one club

WEEK THREE:

☐ Has been contacted by club head and plans on attending one meeting (knows location of meeting)

WEEK FOUR/FIVE:

☐ Midterms reviewed/discussed with student

☐ Midterms reviewed/discussed with parents

☐ Respond to any academic red flags

☐ Communicate above (dorm head/DOS / parents)

☐ Document above

"Help! I Need Somebody"

Suggestions for advisers with students who are struggling academically:

More likely than not, at some point during the school year, advisers will find one or more of their students struggling with their studies. For most new students, difficulties are usually transitional and transitory; for others, there may be underlying learning differences or placement issues. Without being alarmist, advisers should contact the Dean of Academic Affairs, Study Skills Coordinator, or Academic Support Specialist immediately if they have particular concerns about a student.

Below are suggestions advisers can give to help students organize their time and improve their academic standing. Advisers can pick and choose from this list; what's important is to help students learn what strategies work best *for them*. The list is in no particular order of priority.

Note: Advisers should communicate with parents whenever they have a concern about academic performance. It is also useful to document which particular strategies they are using to assist their advisee(s).

1. Often, students who experience academic difficulty are not managing and budgeting their time effectively. The "Time Wasters/Time Savers" exercise from Chapter Two, page 61, is an excellent resource and tool for advisers to use with students who might need a lesson in time management.

2. Sometimes, students may forget to complete assignments or not have experience with planning long-term projects. Advisers should confirm that an advisee has purchased and knows how to effectively use an assignment book/calendar/agenda. (Planners are often given to all students at the start of school, or when needed, the Dean of Academic Affairs, Study Skills Coordinator, or Academic Support Specialist has resources available for financial-aid students.) More and more students now manage their calendars and to-do lists online, or on their mobile devices.

3. Students often carry their books in a backpack or bag that is over-full and disorganized. Advisers can encourage advisees to clean out their backpack and to pack the backpack before going to bed each night.

4. In order to study effectively, students must have a neat, clean place to work. Advisers can remind students to keep their rooms clean and to maintain an area that is neat and organized and always available to be used for study. Some students study best away from their room and the distractions it holds. Advisers can suggest that both boarding and day students find their spot and make it a habit, whether it's a quiet area in their dorm, their home, or at the school or local library.

5. Some students do not know how to organize the volume of material handed out in class, as well as their old tests, or notes. Advisers can help those students by encouraging them to create a file system. Divide a box large enough to hold file folders upright into sections—one for each subject. During the school year as chapters or units are completed, put all notes, handouts, quizzes, and tests organized by subject, into the proper section.

6. Most schools have an extensive and effective peer tutoring program, in which students help their fellow students in specific subject areas. Advisers should contact the Dean of Academic Affairs, Study Skills Coordinator, or Academic Support Specialist to get specific information about how to help an advisee set up peer tutoring.

7. Often, poor academic performance is related to poor habits— whether in sleep hygiene, nutrition, or some emotional stress. The school nurse, school counselor, or health center staff are available to counsel students in these areas, or to assist advisers to do so.

Control What You Can and Delete the Rest!

Overview and Suggested Use:

My experience has been that students can fret and stress over things that are either entirely or mostly out of their control. One way that I have been able to reduce my advisees' stress and increase their focus on what is important (to them) is to ask the simple questions, "What do I control?" and "How can I improve it?" I also have them list things in their lives that they do not control and I tell them to "delete" those things.

Discussion Prompts/Tips:

Sometimes I have my advisees write out the things they feel they can't control on a separate piece of paper, and then tear it up and throw it away.

Advisers should be cautious and observant for advisees who feel nothing is in their control. If that occurs, it is important *not* to have the group share their findings. Advisers should meet with those advisees individually.

Materials:

Pens/pencils

1 copy of each exercise for each student in the group

Advisee folders (Advisee folders are described in the Intro)

Time:

Writing time: 7 – 10 minutes per exercise

Discussion time: this exercise is best discussed as a group so that students can hear one another's study strategies.

> *"No man is fit to command another that cannot command himself."*
> – William Penn

Control What You Can and Delete the Rest!

List a few things that are beyond your control, but that you have to deal with every day. (Example: the weather)

List a few things that are out of your control, but that you worry about. (Examples: the weather, the economy)

List some things about school that are out of your control, but that you deal with every day. (Examples: the lunch menu, what time homeroom is)

List a few simple things that you do control. (Examples: how I comb my hair, what shoes I wear, what ringtone is on my phone)

List some things at school that you do control. (Examples: how diligently you approach your studies, how hard you practice for the band)

Write a response to this prompt: from the above list of things that you *do not* control—how can you "delete" them from your daily worry by working around them? (Example: I could check the weather before class and wear a raincoat on rainy days.)

Write a response to this prompt: from the above list of things that you *do* control—how can you gain even more control? (Example: I practice for the band quite a bit, but I could ask the director or the band mates to practice with me.)

Atmosphere

Academic/Study Skills

Overview and Suggested Use:

Study habits have changed; when I was in school, homework had to be done at a desk in a quiet room alone. Today, the teen brain 'toggles' between screen and page, music and silence, bed and desk. It may be that there is no best atmosphere in which to study, and certainly today's teens are compiling a mountain of anecdotal evidence suggesting that individual preference trumps tradition. If indeed there is no one "right way" to study, instead individuals should find the study environment that works best for them.

Discussion Prompts/Tips:

This exercise is best discussed as a group so that students can hear one another's study strategies. Advisers should resist (as hard as it will be!) trying to encourage advisees to adopt traditional study habits and allow advisees to really discover what works *for them*.

Materials:

Pens/pencils

1 copy of each exercise for each student in the group

Advisee folders (Advisee folders are described in the Intro)

Time:

Writing time: 7 – 10 minutes.

Discussion time: 15 – 20 minutes

Rhythm and Flow

Complete the following:

I study best when...

I do my best work at...(my desk, on the bed, in the library, etc.)

Before I begin to study I need the following items...

Before I begin to study I need to do the following things...

I have noticed that when I have a lot of work I need to...

I prefer to do my homework at...

When I am busy, I manage my stress by...

I prefer to do my homework in the following order...

I like to get my work done ahead of time and this is how I do that...

I get the results that I am happy with when I...

Silver-Bullet Strategies for Nailing Exams

Academic/Study Skills

Overview and Suggested Use:

Many schools have some type of final exam or cumulative exam in all subjects. These are challenging for all students, but some students struggle on these exams more than others, and many new students have little or no experience with them. These exercises are designed to help advisers show advisees how to divide and conquer the end-of-the-term exams. They include some simple tips for advisees, as well as a schedule to be filled out by the student. I adapted this exercise from Beth Hansard, the exceptionally talented Study Skills Coordinator at Baylor School, in Chattanooga, TN.

The second exercise, "Exam Week Preparation," is from Blair Academy, in Blairstown, New Jersey.

It is worth noting that most schools, whether institutionally or through individual teachers or departments, hold some sort of study session for semester tests. The planner below includes a slot where advisers can help advisees schedule time to attend those sessions.

Materials:

Paper copies of the following with additions or deletions based on the policies, practices, and culture of your school.

Mrs. Hansard's Sanity–Restoring Strategies for Cumulative Semester Exams

1. Organize old notes and tests and the study area (room)
2. Divide the material into manageable parts
3. Set up strategies to review (note cards, reading annotations, etc.)
4. Map out a daily schedule for the two weeks prior to the test(s)
5. Review/Study—this is up to the student (we simply make sure the environment is conducive for them to do so…)

Sanity Planner for Exam Study

Exam/Help Schedule

	EXTRA HELP SESSION	EXAM
Sunday		
Monday		
Tuesday		
Wednesday		
Thursday		
Friday		

FRIDAY	SATURDAY	SUNDAY
8 a.m.	8 a.m.	8 a.m.
9	9	9
10	10	10
11	11	11
12	12	12
1 p.m.	1 p.m.	1 p.m.
2	2	2
3	3	3
4	4	4
5	5	5
6	6	6
7	7	7
8	8	8
9	9	9
10	10	10
11	11	11
12	12	12

MONDAY	TUESDAY	WEDNESDAY	THURSDAY	FRIDAY
8 a.m.	8 a.m.	8 a.m.	8 a.m.	8 a.m.
9	9	9	9	9
10	10	10	10	10
11	11	11	11	11
12	12	12	12	12
1 p.m.	1 p.m.	1 p.m.	1 p.m.	1 p.m.
2	2	2	2	
3	3	3	3	
4	4	4	4	
5	5	5	5	
6	6	6	6	
7	7	7	7	
8	8	8	8	
9	9	9	9	
10	10	10	10	
11	11	11	11	

Academic / Study Skills

Exam Week Preparation

DECIDE ON 3 CONCRETE GOALS to prepare for exams over the weekend *before* exams:
(Examples: making vocabulary note cards, organizing binders, reviewing chapter tests, study
groups, etc.)

1.

2.

3.

COME UP WITH 1 QUESTION FOR EACH CLASS that you will ask each teacher on
review day.

1.

2.

3.

4.

5.

6.

STUDY SCHEDULE & EXAM WEEK: (*Note: When is the last day of regular classes? When is the review day?*) Use a different color pen/marker for each exam and exam study time, blocking out the exams and study time on this schedule. Remember to study approximately 4 hours for each 2-hour test. Block out enough time for projects/papers, study sessions, off-campus commitments, packing your dorm room, etc.

Saturday	Sunday	REVIEW DAY	EXAMS	EXAMS	EXAMS
8 a.m.	8 a.m.	1st Period 8:00 – 8:50	8:30 – 10:30 **English**	8:30 – 10:30 **Math**	8:30 – 10:30 **Science**
9 a.m.	9 a.m.	2nd Period 8:55 – 9:45			
10 a.m.	10 a.m.	3rd Period 9:50 – 10:40			
11 a.m.	11 a.m.	4th Period 10:45 – 11:35			
Lunch	Lunch	5th Period 11:40 – 12:30	Lunch	Lunch	Lunch
1 p.m.	1 p.m.	Lunch	1:00 – 3:00 **Language**	1:00 – 3:00 **History**	1:00 – 3:00 **Conflict**
2 p.m.	2 p.m.	6th Period 1:15 – 2:05			
3 p.m.	3 p.m.	7th Period 2:10 – 3:00			
4 p.m.	4 p.m.	4 p.m.			
5 p.m.	5 p.m.	5 p.m.			**BREAK**
Dinner	Dinner	Dinner	Dinner	Dinner	
7 p.m.	7 p.m.	7 p.m.	7 p.m.	7 p.m.	
8 p.m.	8 p.m.	8 p.m.	8 p.m.	8 p.m.	
9 p.m.	9 p.m.	9 p.m.	9 p.m.	9 p.m.	
10 p.m.	10 p.m.	10 p.m.	10 p.m.	10 p.m.	
Sleep	Sleep	Sleep	Sleep	Sleep	

What do Smart Kids Know?

Overview and Suggested Use:

This exercise is actually four exercises in one. I have used it with great success by simply changing the wording from, What Do Smart Kids Know? to What Do Smart Kids Do? to How Do Smart Kids Study? to How Do Student Leaders Lead?

The exercise encourages students to think about steps they can take to be a "smart" student, to improve their study skills, or to flex their leadership muscles.

I place this exercise at the beginning of the book as it is a good way for advisers and advisees to initiate conversations about achievement, study skills/habits, and leadership, but it can also be used at any point during the year.

Once students create an exhaustive list, I often have them group the list by themes and write those themes within the circle.

Discussion Prompts/Tips:

This is an easy to moderate exercise and helps students look at 'big picture' ideas. I have included a few examples from my own advisee group. Simply have the advisee group brainstorm for a few minutes about what smart students know or do, how they study, or how student leaders lead. After a three- or four-minute brainstorm, have them write their responses in their circle. Then, compile the responses into one "group" circle. On occasion, bring the group circle out and remind advisees what they identified as attributes and actions of smart students and leaders.

The follow up for this exercise is to ask: "OK, now that we know what 'smart kids know,' how do we ensure that those things are incorporated into your daily routine?"

Materials:

Pens/pencils

1 copy of the exercise for each student in the group

Advisee folders (Advisee folders are described in the Intro)

Time:

Writing time: 15 minutes.

Discussion time: unlimited.

"High expectations are the key to everything."
– Sam Walton

Adjustment / Transition / Role in School

Academic / Study Skills

Examples of "Group" Circles

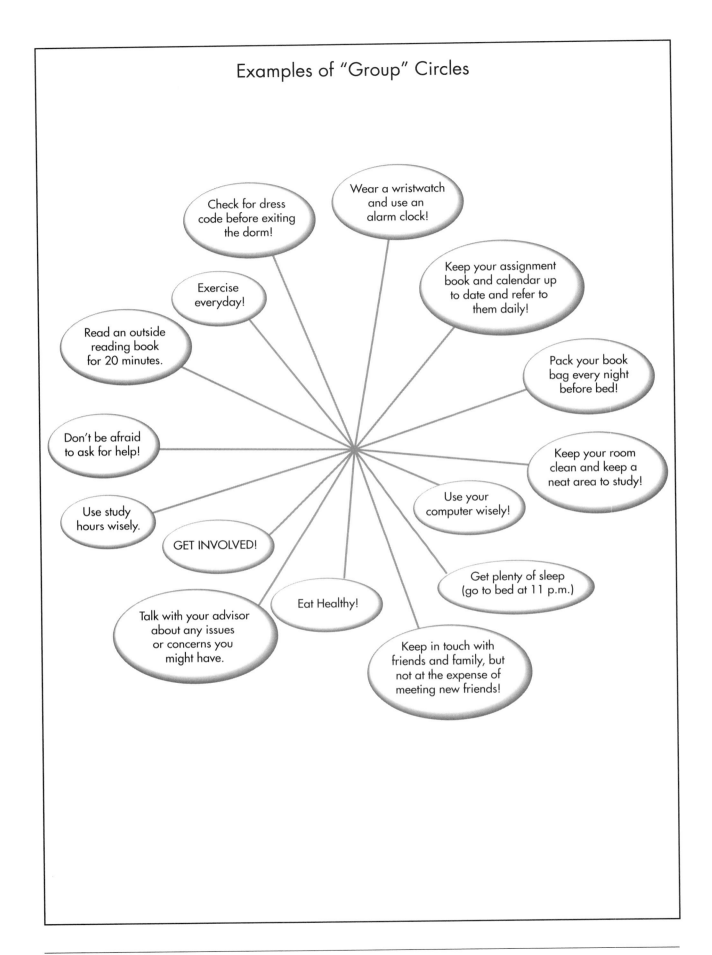

Circle of Choices

ACADEMICS

Take Intiative

Know/Take Advantage
of Resources

Attendance (Go to Class)

Organization/Time Management

Participation in School
Life and at Harkness Table

COMMUNITY

Learn to Make Choices

Abide by Rules

Respect Self & Others

Value Differences

Check Email, Phone, PO Daily

Use Technology Wisely

Be Involved

SELF-CARE

Open Mindedness

Try Something New

Communicate with/Seek
Feedback from Teachers

Sleep Adequately

Develop and Review
Long Term Academic Goals

Eat Well Balanced Meals

Exercise Regularly

Maintain Good Personal Hygiene
and Good Personal Space

Manage Your Money

Develop Spiritual Self

Maintain Personal Traditions

Seek Help for Emotional/
Medical Needs

Seek and Make New Friends

Balance Work and Play

Balance Home
and Campus Life

CHAPTER 2

Exercises, Assignments, and Worksheets for the Fall Semester

This chapter contains ready-to-use worksheets and activities for 9th, 10th, 11th and 12th graders for the fall term. The exercises are appropriate for both new and returning students.

Each exercise has a specific, described goal, but to summarize, the overall plan is as follows:

- Exercises for 9th grade advisees help them begin to set academic and personal goals.

- Exercises for 10th, 11th, and 12th graders help students define excellence for themselves, and outline steps they can take to achieve this excellence.

- Exercises for 11th and 12th graders encourage students to begin to clarify their own values and define who they are for themselves.

> "If you pursue evil with pleasure, the pleasure passes away and the evil remains; If you pursue good with labor, the labor passes away but the good remains."
>
> – Cicero

Coke or Pepsi?

Group Dynamics/
Social Development

Overview and Suggested Use:

Managing the group dynamics and building cohesion and friendships within an advisee group help new and returning students feel at ease. Like team building, members need to know they can rely on one another; that they can rely on teammates, and that their teammates can rely on them. One way to do this is to break the ice and to get students talking about their likes and dislikes.

This simple exercise is designed to get students moving a little bit, laughing a little bit more, and sharing a few things about themselves.

The adviser should clear a space large enough for the group to be able to spread out. Mark with tape or chalk a line down the middle of the space. Have all of the students stand on the line to begin. Read from the list below pointing to one side of the room for the left side of the page and to the other for the right side of the page—students should move to the side of their preference. No student should stand in the middle after a set of words has been read. Watch as they move back and forth when you call out different sets of words.

Discussion Prompts/Tips:

After 10 minutes of reading sets of words, stop and gather the group together. Ask them to talk about the experience. Be sure to point out how infrequently one student stood alone on one side of the room. It is good to note that even with the most simple day-to-day activities and preferences, almost always there were at least two people from the group who liked the same things. All students, young and old, wonder if they will be able to meet people who have similar interests. This exercise visually demonstrates to students the fact that there are other people like them in their advisee group (and at their school!). You'd be surprised how many friendships blossom from such simple preferences.

Materials:

A copy of the list below, with additions or deletions as needed

Time:

Activity time: 7–10 minutes

Discussion time: 15–20 minutes

Coke or Pepsi?

Coke?	Pepsi?
Sandals?	Barefeet?
Tennis Shoes?	Sneakers?
Bagel?	Oatmeal?
Powerade?	Gatorade?
Jacob?	Edward?
Doritos — Cool Ranch?	Original?
Sailboat?	Powerboat?
Yahoo?	Gmail?
Skiing?	Surfing?
Hip Hop?	Country?
Hoagie?	Sub?
DoDA?	WoW?
Pizza Hut?	Dominoes?
Droid?	iPhone?
Red?	Blue?
Hiking?	Biking?
Convertible?	Truck?
Bing?	Google?
Turkey?	Ham?
Chemistry?	Biology?
Dogs?	Cats?
Stairs?	Elevators?
Glasses?	Contacts?
Tea?	Coffee?
Mac?	PC?

Treasure/Scavenger Hunt

Group Dynamics/
Social Development

Adjustment/Transition/
Role in School

Overview and Suggested Use:

Every orientation that I have ever experienced—whether as participant, leader, or observer—has included some form of a "Treasure/Scavenger Hunt." There's a reason for this. The expeditions enable students to accomplish a number of important things in an effective and fun manner. Treasure hunters learn their way around campus, meet school staffers who can help and support them, and share a bonding experience with fellow advisees. The quests can also provide older, more experienced students an opportunity to practice leadership skills.

There are as many ways to set up treasure/scavenger hunts as there are schools and advisers. I prefer to have a hunt that has students find items, etc., that answer particular questions about the school. I like to allot a minimum of 60 minutes for a treasure/scavenger hunt, longer if possible. I allow for 5–10 minutes of planning and preparation, 30–45 minutes of actually hunting, 5–10 minutes of reassembling, and then 5–10 minutes of small group discussion and "show and tell."

Taking advantage of today's mobile technology, I always have student groups take pictures with their handheld devices and send them to one person who can assemble them into a slideshow or similar presentation. Technology is changing so fast that I have recently had each group produce a short video of their treasure/scavenger hunt. I have each group report back on why they chose certain pictures, scenes, or items.

For a treasure/scavenger hunt, I break whatever group I am working with into smaller groups: usually 6–8 students works well, with at least one older, or more experienced student in each group.

Following are some treasure/scavenger hunt themes I have used with great success.

SWAK! (Sealed with a Kiss)

Every school has a seal or motto. The seal usually has some type of picture, quote, or symbol that attempts to represent the founding principles of the school. The motto of a school is typically an inspiring phrase (often in Latin) that encapsulates the school's mission or values.

Encourage the groups to have a brief conversation about what the creators of the seal or motto intended when they set about their task. Then, have the students go and find examples that demonstrate the motto or seal.

Mission Possible!

Although this treasure/scavenger hunt is similar to the school seal/motto one, I use a slightly different approach with mission statements. I make sure that the group spends a few minutes discussing mission statements in general — how they are written, and what their purposes are — because at some point in the future advisees will be writing mission statements of their own.

Did You Hear the One About...

Some treasure/scavenger hunt can lead students to destinations by using hints or riddles. These types of treasure/scavenger hunts are particularly effective at encouraging collaborative work among group members.

Pop Quiz

A quiz treasure/scavenger hunt is a variation of the 'hints and riddles' treasure/scavenger hunt. Advisees are led to destinations by a quiz. Again, group problem-solving is emphasized.

Calling All Famous Alumni

Every school has some number of famous alums. Advisers can help advisees feel more connected to the school and its history by creating a treasure/scavenger hunt that highlights the famous alums of the school. (Advisers should try to be sure that both genders and as many races, religions, cultures are represented on the list.)

Group Dynamics/
Social Development

Adjustment/Transition/
Role in School

Treasure/Scavenger Hunt (continued)

Photo Opp: What is the "Essence" of the School?

My former colleague, Michael McBrien, the head of school at TASIS England, found this question worked well as a prompt for a treasure/scavenger hunt that he ran with adults on his senior administrative team. I have since used it in class and with advisee groups with great success. I have them go out and take pictures of what they feel symbolizes the essence of the school and report back to the entire group.

What Makes the School "Excellent"?

This prompt encourages students to seek evidence of excellence at the school. My experience, however, is that they get into a very positive discussion about what excellence really means and how it is defined by different people, in different areas (academics, athletics, leadership, arts, etc.).

Follow the Paper Trail

At one time or another, each student will need to interact with or receive assistance from each office on campus. Advisers can set up a treasure/scavenger hunt during which advisee groups visit each office to obtain overviews or descriptive hand-outs, and perhaps meet a few staffers. When doing this type of treasure/scavenger hunt in the beginning of the year, I send students only to the offices that they will be using during the first four to six weeks of school, so as not to overwhelm anyone.

Thoughts on My School: Then and Now

This is a good prompt for a treasure/scavenger hunt for new students. This theme encourages new students to discuss with their peers what they especially liked about the school during the admissions process and then to clarify what they like about the school now.

"If You Build It..."

Advisers can create a treasure/scavenger hunt in which the group must create something at the end of the hunt. The nature of the final creation is completely up to the treasure/scavenger hunt organizer. A school with an outdoor education program, for example, might have the students gather materials to build a shelter. At Exeter, I have used this treasure/scavenger hunt to have students build a "Harkness" table, as it is central to our school's pedagogy.

White Pages...

When I set up a "White Pages" treasure hunt I give students a list of important people on campus (the head custodian, the secretary in the principal's office, the secretary in the gym, the librarian, etc.) and have them find each one. I work with these folks ahead of time to make sure that they have a single sheet of paper explaining their area, their role, and anything else they feel is important for students to know.

On Your Mark, Get Set...

In general, I avoid creating competitions between new students in order to help them assimilate more naturally with the group, however, when working with more experienced groups, advisers can turn treasure/scavenger hunt into races that pit two or more teams against each other. Each stop in a treasure/scavenger hunt is worth a certain number of points, and bonus points can be awarded if a group completes a task and records it with a picture.

Goal Setting

Values Clarification

Group Dynamics/
Social Development

Adjustment/Transition/
Role in School

Three Positive Things That Have Happened Since School Started

Overview and Suggested Use:

The beginning of school can be a difficult time for all students. New teachers, new approaches, new routines take time to get used to, especially for younger students. The purpose of this exercise is threefold: to get students to focus on the positive things that have happened at school; to restate goals from the summer; and to specifically identify adult and peer allies. Have advisees write responses to the questions below. Have them spend a few minutes discussing with their neighbor three positive things that have happened and one area of frustration since the beginning of school. Sometimes, it is good to have them report out any common themes.

Discussion Prompts/Tips:

Most students will put down achievement-based goals or outcome goals: in other words, they'll write, "I want to get straight A's," or "I want to play on the varsity team." As discussed in the Introduction, it is our job as advisers to encourage students to set performance or process goals instead. That is, encourage advisees to write goals such as, "I will go to every help session my math teacher offers." Or, "I will lift weights and run every day to prepare for the season." Setting measurable, achievable goals with specific timeframes and parameters gives students the best chance at establishing a positive feedback loop, not to mention the thrill and satisfaction of accomplishment.

Materials:

Pens/pencils

1 copy of the exercise for each student in the group

Advisee folders (Advisee folders are described in the Intro)

Time:

Writing time: 10–12 minutes

Discussion time: unlimited

> *"Don't ask what the world needs. Ask what makes you come alive, and go do it. Because what the world needs is people who have come alive."* —Howard Thurman

Three Positive Things That Have Happened Since School Started

1.

2.

3.

Source(s) of Frustration Since Arriving:

The Student(s) That Know(s) Me Best Is/Are—And Why?

The Adult(s) at School That Know(s) Me Best Is/Are—And Why?

Three Academic Goals That I Have For the Next Month (Until Midterms):
1.

2.

3.

Three Personal Goals That I Have For the Next Month (Until Midterms):
1.

2.

3.

What Can Your Adviser Do to Help You Adjust to the New School Year & Meet Your Goals?

[For Boarding Students] How Comfortable Do You Feel Living in Your Dorm?

A Weekly Return on a Daily Investment
How do You Spend Your 168 Hours Each Week?

Overview and Suggested Use:

Teenagers can spend an enormous amount of time on activities that are unrelated to their goals. Sometimes it is helpful for them to actually see how they spend their time written down in black and white. These three exercises require that students be thoughtful about where in their day they waste time and what steps they can take to turn wasted time into productive activities that will move them toward their goals. The exercises can be done together or individually, depending on the group and each student's particular time management skills. The exercises can be used in any order—each challenges the student to do a self-evaluation. Although these exercises are listed in the 9th grade chapter, they have relevance during each year of school.

Discussion Prompts/Tips:

Ask students to think about their "screen time"—time in front of a computer, phone, or TV in which they are not doing something academically related. If they give honest responses, they might be shocked by the math!

Materials:

Pens/pencils

1 copy of each exercise for each student in the group

Advisee folders (Advisee folders are described in the Intro)

Time:

Writing time: 7–10 minutes per exercise

Discussion time: these exercises are best discussed on an individual basis with each advisee if time permits; however, a general discussion amongst the group often shows that students are wasting their time on similar activities. Advisers can brainstorm with the group to help them come up with strategies to use their time in concert with their goals.

> *"The fight is won or lost far away from witnesses — behind the lines, in the gym, and out there on the road, long before I dance under those lights."* —Mohammed Ali

Time Wasters/Time Savers

Everyone wastes time every once in a while, but we need to be careful and not waste too much or not let poor time management keep us from achieving our goals. List four ways you misuse your time. (Examples: phone, TV, Facebook, video games, IM, etc.) Beside each, write down what *you* could do to minimize these time eaters.

We all want to be part of group and to hang out with friends, but sometimes, we also need to break away from the group and work on reaching our goals. Note three instances in which your time is "wasted" by others, including situations beyond your control, such as dealing with high-maintenance friends or dorm issues (for boarding students) that don't really have a direct bearing on you. Then list how you might reclaim that time.

List three areas where you might be able to save, optimize, or better use time. For example— riding on buses to away games is a waste of time: you could purchase a book light to study while you rode.

Time Management — Personal Assessment

Think of a time when you finished your homework or a project on time and completed it to a level you were pleased with. What steps do you take?

Did you set a time to study or work on the project each day?

Did you review the syllabus or assignment and break the task(s) down into smaller ones?

Did you set a personal deadline for each task?

Did you follow a daily planner?

If you got behind on a part of the project, how did you manage to catch up?

Take a minute to review your answers from the above; the things that you did do would be considered strengths and the things that you did not do would be considered weaknesses.

Based on your strengths, what strategies should you do more of?

Based on your weaknesses, what strategies should you employ to turn them into strengths?

168 Hours

How do you spend your time each week? Below is a list of items most of us take part in on a daily basis. Next to each item, indicate how many hours you spend each week completing it.

	SUNDAY	MONDAY	TUESDAY	WEDNESDAY	THURSDAY	FRIDAY	SATURDAY
Sleeping							
In Class							
Sports/Extra-curricular							
Working							
Homework							
Religious Services							
Eating							
Other							
Total							

Add all the totals together _____

Subtract your total amount from 168. How many do you have remaining? _____

Now think of how many hours you spend doing recreational activities such as IM, computer, Facebook, Twitter, online games, talking on the phone, watching television. _____

Now think about how many hours you spend on your homework each day. _____

Does that seem sufficient to meet your academic goals?

If not, what can you spend less time on from the above list so that you can add more hours to your academic work?

Divide and Conquer

Goal Setting

Academic/Study Skills

Overview and Suggested Use:

Part of time management is prioritizing tasks and keeping track of what needs to be done and when. Although this exercise may seem simple to adults, I have found that the concept of making a list and sticking to it is foreign to teens.

It is important for advisers to teach advisees the difference between "projects," "assignments," or "work;" and "tasks." The former are the things that need to be accomplished (end results), whereas tasks are what have to be done to complete the project, assignment, or work (the means to the ends).

Discussion Prompts/Tips:

This exercise is listed in the 9th Grade chapter under the Fall Semester section; however it can be used for any grade at any time.

There are many online task managers that students can use or purchase; some are downloadable to handheld mobile devices, as well. A few to consider are Evernote, Sticky Notes, and Memo to Me.

I try to get students to repeat the mantra, "Divide and Conquer," when faced with homework and other school-related tasks.

There is not a great deal of discussion to be had with this exercise.

Materials:

Pens/pencils

1 copy of the exercise for each student in the group

Advisee folders (Advisee folders are described in the Intro)

Time:

Writing time: 10–12 minutes

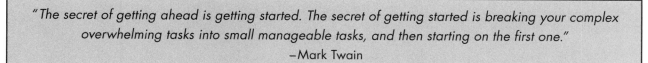

"The secret of getting ahead is getting started. The secret of getting started is breaking your complex overwhelming tasks into small manageable tasks, and then starting on the first one."
–Mark Twain

Divide and Conquer

Think of a large assignment or a project that you have to complete (i.e.: finish the lab report, or clean my room) and write it here:

Write down the steps involved in completing the work or project—these steps are tasks. Divide the tasks into the smallest parts possible. (i.e.: get paper for the lab report)

Go back and prioritize the list of tasks by when they need to be completed. You can prioritize the list by re-writing it with the most important tasks at the top, or by numbering the tasks from most crucial to the least crucial. Some individuals also color code the tasks—for example, red being the highest priority, green being the least crucial.

Begin work on the task that you have deemed the top priority.

Group Dynamics/
Social Development

Academic/Study Skills

Adjustment/Transition/
Role in School

What do You Bring to the Team?

Overview and Suggested Use:

Self-awareness, especially awareness of one's strengths, is crucial to academic and social success. Many new or younger students lose sight of why they were accepted to a school in the first place, or forget that they were ever a good student when they first experience the academic challenges of a new school. This exercise helps students re-focus on what their strengths are and how they can add to and lead a class/team, a student club or, in the case of boarding students, a dorm.

Discussion Prompts/Tips:

Sometimes, it is helpful to get the students to think about their own strengths by first asking them about the strengths of other leaders. Ask simple questions like: "What made Michael Jordan a leader?" or "Name a political figure you respect; in your opinion, why is that person a good leader?"

Materials:

Pens/pencils

1 copy of the exercise for each student in the group

Advisee folders (Advisee folders are described in the Intro)

Time:

Writing time: 7–10 minutes

Discussion time: brief—this early in the school year students are usually unwilling to talk about their strengths in front of their peers.

What do You Bring to the Team?

Describe the skills and qualities that make *you* effective in groups and as a leader. (Be specific.)

List three ways that you can effectively work with and support your classmates to accomplish difficult tasks and succeed:

1.

2.

3.

List three ways that you can use your leadership qualities to give back to the community:

1.

2.

3.

Adjustment / Transition / Role in School

Academic / Study Skills

Group Dynamics/Social Development

Father Pusateri's "Be A Good Kid"

A NOTE TO READERS

Father Pusateri was a Chaplain and a Religious Studies teacher at my high school, Boston College High School. As I mention in the Forward, during one of our first classes, he gave us a version of this exercise, which I have never forgotten. Whenever I do this exercise, I tell my group about Father Pusateri. When I need help with my own students, I turn back to what I learned in high school… I can only hope that some of my advisees do the same in the future!

Overview and Suggested Use:

All schools have a student handbook, code of conduct, or honor code; in a very simple way, this exercise asks students to reflect about how they can live those codes in their everyday lives. This exercise is excellent for helping students to become more thoughtful about their behavior, both at and away from school. The exercise asks students to define "goodness" for themselves and to be thoughtful about how they can change (or continue) the culture to one of "goodness" at their school. The exercise also helps students identify the adults at school to whom they might turn for help in being "good."

Have the students read the exercise and for one or two minutes simply think about their responses. Once they have quietly reflected, have them write down answers to the Prompts/Tips on the page. Allow written responses to come in any format—note, bullets, paragraphs, stream of consciousness—as the written response is only for the student's and adviser's eyes. After the students have had a chance to respond, return to the Prompts/Tips to lead a discussion among your advisees.

Discussion Prompts/Tips:

Ask the students:

So, what does it mean to *you* to be a "good kid?"

How are good kids viewed or treated at our school?

Without naming them, do you know any good kids? Why do you define them as good kids?

I asked each of you what the adults at our school could do to help you be a good kid. Without using any names, is there at least one adult you feel you could turn to for support? What is it about that adult that makes you feel like you could approach him/her?

What are some specific steps you can take to help your friends be "good kids?"

Materials:

Pens/pencils

1 copy of the exercise for each student in the group

Advisee folders (Advisee folders are described in the Intro)

Time:

Writing time: 10–12 minutes

Discussion time: unlimited.

Father Pusateri's "Be A Good Kid"

Some words to live by from some of the world's foremost philosophers:

An uninspiring person believes according to what he achieves. An aspiring person achieves according to what he believes. – Sri Chinmoy

It is sometimes frightening to observe the success which comes even to the outlaw with a polished technique... But I believe we must reckon with character in the end, for it is as potent a force in world conflict as it is in our own domestic affairs. It strikes the last blow in any battle. – Philip D. Reed

"Be a good kid!" ("Or I'll kick your butt!") – Grandma Morrissey

Please read and reflect on the following questions and write your response in the space provided. (This will only be seen by you and your adviser, but you'll be expected to talk about your responses with the group.)

What does it mean to be a "good kid?"

What can I do to be a "good kid?"

What can the faculty (or my adviser) do to help me be a "good kid?"

Is being a "good kid" at my school different from being a "good kid" in the "real world?"

How can I help other students around me be "good kids?"

What's Your Bucket List?

Values Clarification

Adjustment/Transition/
Role in School

Overview and Suggested Use:

This is a simple exercise that can be used with any age group at any time of the year. The crucial step for advisers is to follow up on the list. Have the students complete the exercise and then check in with them a week or two later to see how they are doing on their list.

Discussion Prompts/Tips:

I often have my advisees write down their list and then come back to me two or three weeks later and journal on what they have been able to check off. These journals are usually private.

Materials:

Pens/pencils

1 copy of the exercise for each student in the group

Advisee folders (Advisee folders are described in the Intro)

Time:

Writing time: 10–12 minutes

Discussion time: unlimited.

My Bucket List!

Write down five small (but appropriate) things that you have always wanted to do but have not yet done.

1.

2.

3.

4.

5.

Write down how you might accomplish these five small (but appropriate) things this week.

Be prepared to tell me if you were able to complete the list and what it felt like.

Character and
Leadership
Development

Values Clarification

You Bet Your Assets!

Overview and Suggested Use:

Successful students can articulate what they are good at and what their strengths are. Savvy students can also quickly articulate what they need to work on. This exercise helps advisees put down on paper and discuss their strengths. This exercise also helps students think about how they celebrate their successes.

Discussion Prompts/Tips:

As advisees discuss their written responses, advisers can listen objectively to their subjective responses and help to positively reframe them. Sometimes, it is better to do this reframing individually with advisees.

Materials:

Pens/pencils

1 copy of the exercise for each student in the group

Advisee folders (Advisee folders are described in the Intro)

Time:

Writing time: 8 – 10 minutes

Discussion time: unlimited.

You Bet Your Assets!

What is the one thing you are better at than anyone else?

What about your personality do people find charming?

What lesson(s) have you learned the hard way?

How do you celebrate success?

Values Clarification

Character and Leadership Development

The Recipe of Me

Values Clarification

Group Dynamics/
Social Development

Adjustment/Transition/
Role in School

Overview and Suggested Use:

This exercise asks, quite literally, "What are you made of?" I have used this exercise with great success to help students think about what it is that makes them who they are. The exercise is a bit reminiscent of something done in grade school or middle school health class, but my experience has been that high school students still enjoy it, too.

Discussion Prompts/Tips:

Have students list the ingredients that they are comprised of, for example: I am 2 cups basketball player, 2 cups big sister, ½ cup singer, mixed with one part Student Council member and 1 cup Calculus whiz with a dash of surfer girl for flavor.

Sometimes, it helps students to think about this exercise in terms of a single type of food. I have used layered foods, or foods where one can see all of the ingredients, such as cookies, pizza, tacos, or a big burger. Some students, especially in the lower grades, enjoy drawing a picture of their chosen food or completed recipe.

Materials:

Pens/pencils, maybe crayons/colored markers

1 copy of the exercise for each student in the group

Advisee folders (Advisee folders are described in the Intro)

Time:

Writing time: 12 – 15 minutes

Discussion time: unlimited.

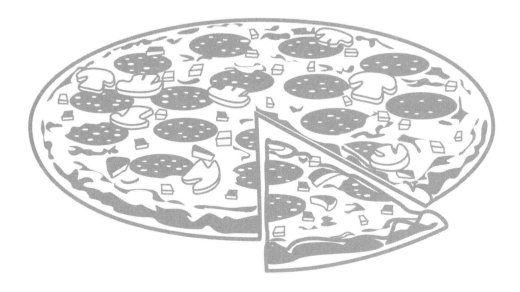

The Recipe of Me

We are all made up of different interests, passions, and abilities. Each of us is affected by our particular experiences, as well as the relationships we have with others and with ourselves.

Take a minute and think about the things you really like to do, the things that you are good at, and the people you like to be around—both family and friends. Think about the things that make you different and full of flavor.

Now list the ingredients that you think you are made of; for example: "I am 2 cups basketball player, 2 cups big sister, ½ cup singer, mixed with one part Student Council member and 1 cup Calculus whiz with a dash of surfer girl for flavor."

Another way to think about this is to answer the question: "If I were a pizza, what would my toppings be?" Or: "If I were a taco, what ingredients would be between the shell?"

Fire Drill !!!

Group Dynamics/
Social Development

Adjustment/Transition/
Role in School

Overview and Suggested Use:

In a stressed out, busy, and materialistic world, students often need to be reminded of what is important to them, what they care about, and what they cherish. This is a quick, simple activity that helps students clarify what they value and why. This activity also helps individuals in an advisee group get to know one another better, while also letting the adviser get to know his or her advisees more deeply.

I use this exercise throughout the school year as a fun, quick activity. It is important to remind the advisee group that there will be sharing of personal information during this activity and that they must be respectful and careful as to what details they share outside of the group and how that information is conveyed.

Advisers at boarding schools can actually have the student run to his/her room and grab items and have them bring them back to the group.

An alternative exercise in the same vein is to have students collect their favorite quotes and bring them to a group meeting to share. (This alternative comes in quite handy if you ever plan on writing a workbook!)

Discussion Prompts/Tips:

Sometimes students will "grab" the simple article or possession—encourage them to be thoughtful.

Time:

Writing time: variable

Discussion time: unlimited.

Fire Drill !!!

Just kidding, but try to pretend.

You have 90 seconds to run to your room/house and bring back one item that you would want to save in a real fire. (Be prepared to share the item with the group.)

What item did you bring back?

Why?

Adjustment / Transition / Role in School

Group Dynamics/Social Development

30 Second Commercial

(From *Character and Coaching* by John Yeager, Amy L. Baltzell,
John N. Buxton, Wallace B. Bzdell - National Professional Resources, Inc.
(2001). Used with permission.)

Overview and Suggested Use:

This exercise was shown to me by John Yeager, who teaches at Culver Academy in Culver, Indiana. He uses it when helping individuals develop mission statements, and I have adapted it for advisers with his permission.

It is important for students to assess their social, emotional, and academic behavior and standing in the most objective manner possible. Advisers can help advisees accomplish this by encouraging them to think about how they are viewed through others' eyes.

This exercise asks students to reflect on their time at a school and to think about how they might be perceived from an objective vantage point. Most importantly, this exercise asks students to consider the differences between their own realities and what they think others' perceptions might be, and asks them what specific steps they can take to better align those viewpoints.

Materials:

Pens/pencils

1 copy of the exercise for each student in the group

Advisee folders (Advisee folders are described in the Intro)

Time:

Writing time: 10–12 minutes, although some teenage students might struggle to see themselves through others' eyes and may need more time.

Discussion time: unlimited.

30 Second Commercial

Pretend that the following people have a surprise, unplanned encounter with one another and the question comes up about you and your school. In the spaces below write what you imagine the response would be in each of the following situations:

Your parents meet your best friend's parents at the local grocery store. What do they say about your experience at school so far—academic, social, behavioral?

The director of your old team, organization, club, church group, etc. calls your house and asks how you're doing at school. What will the response be?

You see a tour guide walking past the place where you like to hang out at school. What is the tour guide telling the prospective student about your hangout? What is the student perception of your hangout? What is the adult perception?

Re-read the above statements. On the back of this page discuss the discrepancies (if any) between what people are saying and thinking about your behavior, your social development, your academic achievement, your extracurricular activities, and what is actually happening. How can you help to better inform people of exactly what you're doing here and what you want them to know about you?

Adjustment / Transition / Role in School

Group Dynamics/Social Development

Values Clarification

Character and Leadership Development

Goal Setting

Party Like It's 2029

Goal Setting

Values Clarification

Group Dynamics/
Social Development

Overview and Suggested Use:

As encompassing as their present lives are, it is important for young students to begin to think about what lies ahead. This exercise allows advisers to help students contemplate their futures in a fun, simple way.

Discussion Prompts/Tips:

Advisers can add to the conversation by asking additional, thought-provoking questions such as:

- Who will be president in 2029?

- What will be the most popular book in 2029?

- What sport will be the most watched in 2029?

- How will people get around town in 2029?

- Will humans inhabit other planets in 2029?

- Which governments or countries will be considered 'superpowers' in 2029?

- What technological device will people not be able to live without in 2029?

Materials:

Pens/pencils

1 copy of the exercise for each student in the group

Advisee folders (Advisee folders are described in the Intro)

Time:

Writing time: 10–12 minutes

Discussion time: unlimited.

Party Like It's 2029

I will be _____ years old in 2029.

Each day I will get up in the morning and I _____.

Every night just before I go to bed I _____.

People that I am friends with now and will still be friends with in 2029 are _____
_____ .

Hobbies or activities that I do now that will still be hobbies or activities I do in 2029 are _____
_____
_____ .

By 2029 I will have visited the following countries _____
to see or do _____ .

When I have free time I _____
_____
_____

The one possession that I still have from high school is _____
_____

If someone were to describe me back in high school, what would they say about me?

If someone just met me, how would that person describe me?

Goal Setting

Values Clarification

Group Dynamics/Social Development

Leadership 101

Goal Setting

Character and
Leadership
Development

Values Clarification

Overview and Suggested Use:

Each of us has the potential to be a good leader. This exercise helps younger students recognize their leadership abilities and qualities and encourages them to be thoughtful about how they might expand on those strengths.

Discussion Prompts/Tips:

This is a simple exercise that can be used for any age or grade level. Sometimes students are reticent to discuss their responses. Advisers should read the dynamics of the group before initiating a discussion.

Materials:

Pens/pencils

1 copy of the exercise for each student in the group

Advisee folders (Advisee folders are described in the Intro)

Time:

Writing time: 7 – 10 minutes

Discussion time: unlimited.

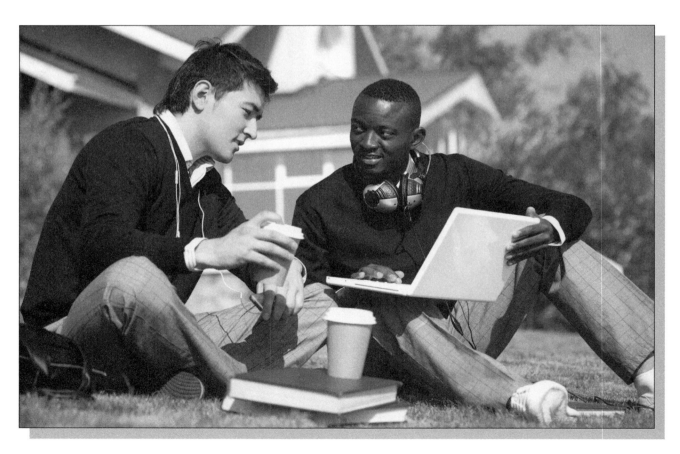

Leadership 101

Write about a time when you helped a friend or family member accomplish something that he or she would not have been able to do without your help. What type of assistance did you give? Was it in the form of advice? Or labor? Did you listen to them or teach them how to do something?

What surprised you about the experience?

What did you enjoy about the experience?

What made you proudest about the experience?

In what areas do you think you can best help people? For example: following the rules, using a computer, practicing music, English class, etc?

How can you put yourself in a position to assist others in the future?

Values Clarification

Character and Leadership
Development

Goal Setting

Goal Setting

Character and
Leadership
Development

Values Clarification

Academic/Study Skills

Overview and Suggested Use:

All students can benefit from being thoughtful, deliberate, and intentional about a few tenets, pillars, or 'commandments' that guide their actions and behaviors. Advisers can assist advisees in clarifying these commandments, and by encouraging them to think about how to put them to use.

Discussion Prompts/Tips:

This can be a challenging writing exercise and is best used with older students. Sometimes it is helpful to give students examples of commandments that are realistic and to list some concrete actions that help achieve the desired goals. For example, a 'commandment' for your life might be: Address people with a smile and a happy greeting! Potential actions might be: In order to address people with a smile and a happy greeting, one has to look up, be aware of his/her surroundings, and not be plugged in with ear buds or cell phones. Another possible action: trying to learn as many people's names as possible.

A 'commandment' for a team that you're on: Hold a meeting at the beginning or end of each practice to check-in with the other team members. Potential useful actions might be explaining why you would like to hold the meeting and asking the coach for permission.

Some teens are hesitant to discuss their commandments in front of others. Advisers should take care to assess the mood of the group before opening it up to discussion.

Materials:

Pens/pencils

1 copy of the exercise for each student in the group

Advisee folders (Advisee folders are described in the Intro)

Time:

Writing time: 15–20 minutes.

"Decide on what you think is right, and stick to it."
–George Elliot

Commandments

Choose three to five "Commandments" for your life; after each, suggest an action you can take to ensure that the commandment is fulfilled.

1.
Action:

2.
Action:

3.
Action:

4.
Action:

5.
Action:

List three to five "Commandments" for the team you are on, a club or organization you belong to (or, for boarding students, the dorm you live in); after each, write an action you can take to ensure that the commandment is fulfilled.

1.
Action:

2.
Action:

3.
Action:

4.
Action:

5.
Action:

Academic / Study Skills

Values Clarification

Character and Leadership Development

Goal Setting

Short Bios

Goal Setting

Character and Leadership Development

Values Clarification

Overview and Suggested Use:

This is a common exercise that many teachers have used over the years. It encourages advisees to think about how they are perceived, and how they would like to be perceived in the present and the future.

Discussion Prompts/Tips:

This can be a very challenging exercise for some students. Sometimes, students, especially teenage boys, are less willing to openly discuss their responses. Advisers should read the mood of their advisees before asking them to share openly.

Materials:

Pens/pencils
1 copy of the exercise for each student in the group
Advisee folders (Advisee folders are described in the Intro)

Time:

Writing time: 15 – 18 minutes
Discussion time: unlimited.

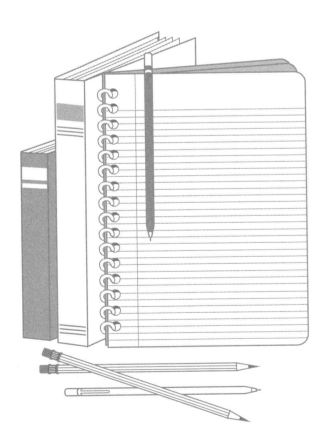

"Don't try to describe the scenery if you've never seen it."
–Jimmy Buffett

Short Bios

Your friends are going to speak about you at graduation. Write what you would like them to say about you in the space below:

A potential employer is interviewing you during your senior year of college; they ask you to write a short biography of yourself. Do it the space below:

Write a letter to your first-born child about your life (up to that point):

You are headed to your 50th high school reunion. Your grandchildren will read a biography of your life. Write what they will say below:

Continue answers on back of sheet

Values Clarification

Character and Leadership Development

Goal Setting

"Sleep is not cumulative, but lack of sleep is!"
S. Chiounard — 1986

Overview and Suggested Use:

The title of this exercise is the first and best lesson I ever received on sleep patterns and how they affect daily life. The lesson came from my college roommate as he encouraged me to retire early during a difficult week filled with papers, labs, and tests.

It doesn't take an experienced educator to know that teen sleep patterns are very different from those of adults. The teen brain is programmed to stay awake later in the evening, and remain asleep later in the morning. Combined with the natural circadian rhythms that make it difficult for teens to settle into restorative sleep are the distractions they have at their fingertips.

This exercise encourages students to think about their sleep habits and to discuss them with their peers and an adult who cares about their success.

Discussion Prompts/Tips:

This exercise is most effective if it is preceded by a 'sleep audit' or 'sleep history' where students record their bedtimes each night, their activities prior to sleep, their wake-up times, whether they were awakened during the night, etc. The audit should be for a minimum of seven days. Experience has shown that allowing students to keep their audit individually, and not in a pre-set form, allows for more complete responses.

Materials:

Pens/pencils

1 copy of the exercise for each student in the group

Advisee folders (Advisee folders are described in the Intro)

Advisees should be reminded to bring the results of their sleep audit with them for reference when completing this exercise.

Time:

Writing time: 10 – 12 minutes (excluding sleep audit)

Discussion time: unlimited.

> *"What you can achieve is not so much determined by your abilities as it is by your choices."*
> –Albus Dumbledore

"Sleep is not cumulative, but lack of sleep is!"
S. Chiounard — 1986

On average, how much sleep (in hours) do you get per night?

How many hours do you think you need? (In other words, are you sleeping enough?)

At what time do you go to bed each night? Does it vary?

Do you sleep in the same place each night? (Some teenagers split time between parents' homes, but wherever you regularly go to bed, do you sleep in the same place each night — not, for example, on the couch some nights, in a bed other nights?)

What do you do before you go to bed? Do you have a pre-bed routine? Do you eat or drink anything before you go to bed?

What helps you fall asleep?

Do you wake up during the night? What wakes you (bathroom, dreams, noise, light, cellphone)?

Do you wake up and need to check Facebook, Twitter, text messages, or emails?

What time do you usually wake up? How do you wake up (cell phone, music, lights, etc.)?

How long after you wake up do you feel fully "functional"? What helps you feel fully functional?

Do you fall asleep during the day?

During the daytime, how do you use the area where you sleep (study, hanging out, sitting)?

What Makes You Happy?

Goal Setting

Character and
Leadership
Development

Values Clarification

Adjustment/Transition/
Role in School

Health/Life Skills

Overview and Suggested Use:

I generated this list of questions after reading Mary Pipher's *Reviving Ophelia*; in it, she suggests adults help students (she was specific about girls) "center" themselves by responding to a series of questions. However, I have found that not all students generate their own goals organically. Often, students' goals are deeply rooted in, or intertwined with, the goals others have had for them, whether tacitly or explicitly stated. The risk is that students' goals, especially goals imposed on them by others, are achievement- or outcome-based, rather than process-based, and that such all-or-nothing stakes might be setting kids up for failure. Only by knowing what really makes them happy and by following their passions will teenagers be able to set goals that are truly their own.

This exercise helps students clarify what makes them most happy and then to state this explicitly.

This exercise is best used with more mature (older) students.

Discussion Prompts/Tips:

Some students may not be comfortable discussing their responses with others. Advisers should open this exercise to discussion only with groups in which members are comfortable with and well known to one another.

Materials:

Pens/pencils

1 copy of the exercise for each student in the group

Advisee folders (Advisee folders are described in the Intro)

Time:

Writing time: 10–12 minutes

Discussion time: variable.

> *"Be Careful, Be Kind, Be Yourself."*
> —Anonymous

What Makes You Happy?

What makes you happy?

What do you want?

How can you close the gap between those two questions?

What is the most important thing you learned today?

Why do you think it was important?

Where were you, whom were you with, and from whom did you learn it?

Was it easy to learn? Why?

In what setting to do you learn best?

How can you ensure that you are in that setting every time you have important work to do?

Put Your Money (and Your Time) Where Your Goals Are!

Goal Setting

Values Clarification

Academic/Study Skills

Overview and Suggested Use:

Getting students to prioritize is not an easy task. This exercise encourages students to prioritize their aspirations and goals in a three-dimensional, tactile way. It demonstrates, in a very visual way, that you need to put resources behind achievement. It works equally well with groups or individual advisees. I learned it from my colleagues in the Exeter Science Department, who used a version of it while planning a new building.

Advisers should start a discussion with the participants and have them brainstorm some specific accomplishments they would like to achieve by their fifth high school reunion. Advisers should then ask students to write down between three and six accomplishments in the allotted space. Next, advisers should give each advisee 20 of the $1 cutouts and 24 of the 1-hour cutouts from below, and have them allocate the amount of time and money they think they'll need to accomplish their goals.

Discussion Prompts/Tips:

This exercise requires some maturity and is best suited for 11th and 12th graders. Advisers should watch the group as they work through assigning their allotted "time" and "money." Be on the lookout for advisees who put "money" but no "time" on any given accomplishment. The two should be in proportion.

Materials:

Pens/pencils

Tape (optional- advisers can have advisees tape their "time" and "money" onto the page and store the page in their advisee folders)

1 copy of the exercise for each student in the group

20 copies of the "$1" below and 24 copies of the "1 Hour" below

Advisee folders (Advisee folders are described in the Intro)

Time:

Writing time: 20 minutes

Discussion time: unlimited.

$1   1 Hour

Put Your Money (and Your Time) Where Your Goals Are!

Think about your fifth high school reunion. Brainstorm between three and six things you would like to have accomplished by that time. The accomplishments can be anything—winning a national chess championship, being accepted to Stanford Law School, becoming the valedictorian of your college class, getting married, etc. Write the accomplishment that you come up with in the numbered squares below, then assign each square a dollar amount and an amount of hours.

1	2
3	4
5	6

In Sync

Overview and Suggested Use:

Today's students understand the term "sync" from an iPod or iPhone very well. This exercise draws a parallel between updating what you carry around all day and what is actually available. It is for more mature students.

Discussion Prompts/Tips:

My experience is that some students may not be comfortable discussing their responses. Advisers should open this exercise to group discussion only when students are comfortable with and know one another well.

Materials:

Pens/pencils

1 copy of the exercise for each student in the group

Advisee folders (Advisee folders are described in the Intro)

Time:

Writing time: 10–12 minutes

Discussion time: variable.

In Sync

Do you own an iPod, iPhone, or MP3 player?

Think about the last time you "synced" your iPod, iPhone, or MP3 player. Did what was on your computer reflect what was stored on the device? What were some of the differences; was the device better after it was synced? Did it hold better music or pictures? Were there old songs that you deleted, new ones that you added? Were you surprised by the updates?

Imagine that you could "sync" yourself—are there parts that would be deleted and others that would be updated? Describe them.

Take a minute and write down the ways that you can "sync your sync" so that your "playlist" is what you want it to be.

Take another minute and write down the names of two adults and two peers whom you think could assist you with this syncing.

The Old College Try

Overview and Suggested Use:

I use this exercise with 11th graders in the late winter or early spring. I usually do this exercise in two meetings as I often have my 11th grade advisees begin this assignment during the first gathering, take the sheet home to complete it, and bring it back for further discussion. Most independent schools have a college counseling office, or individual who works with students during the college process. My experience with advisees is that you can never start too early to help them clarify their thoughts around their list of colleges. I share this exercise with parents as well—it is not unusual for an advisee's list of colleges to be different from that of his/her parents. This exercise helps bridge that conversation. I usually email parents this exercise to give them time to consider these questions themselves, and to also alert them that their son or daughter will be discussing this exercise with them soon. (An example of that email is contained in Chapter 5 section titled, "From In Loco Parentis to Societas Parentis.")

Discussion Prompts/Tips:

This exercise can be done individually or in a group; advisers should be aware of the dynamics within their group to know if advisees are ready to share their college hopes and dreams with their peers.

Materials:

Pens/pencils

1 copy of the exercise for each student in the group

Advisee folders (Advisee folders are described in the Introduction)

Time:

Writing time: 15 – 20 minutes

Discussion time: variable—but usually two separate meetings, often individual meetings

"Life is my college."
–Anonymous

The Old College Try

The college process can be very stressful for students. This exercise helps you to begin to think critically about your college choices.

Break the country into four quadrants—Northeast, Southeast, Northwest, and Southwest. Also consider international (including Canadian) colleges/universities. Write the geographic location(s) where you would like to attend college.

Would you like to attend a large school (over 20,000 undergrads), a medium sized school (10,000–20,000 undergrads), or a small school (fewer than 10,000 undergrads)?

Would you like to attend a "traditional" college or a "non-traditional" one? For the Northeast, a traditional college might be Boston College, and an example of a non-traditional college might be the College of the Atlantic.

Would you like to attend a state university or private university?

Are there colleges/universities that offer specific programs that interest you? (examples: music, art, six-year medical programs)

After completing this exercise, a potential list of colleges to research further should begin to emerge. Take this sheet home and research colleges that align with your chosen criteria above and write down the names of 10–12 colleges that fit the bill. Bring the list to our next meeting.

   Also, please speak with your parents and schedule a tour of a local college or university. Simply taking a tour helps students know better what to expect: where the tour guide will direct you, what other prospective students are wearing, and what kinds of questions they are asking. It might be helpful to tour a state school and a private school to see if there is a different feel to them.

My Life in Music

Values Clarification

Adjustment/Transition/
Role in School

Overview and Suggested Use:

This is a fun exercise that forces advisees to think about their lives in a completely new way. Students should do this exercise on their own. I usually give them a week to complete the CD.

Make sure to listen to each CD, and to read each advisee's list of songs. I try to have a short, individual conversation with each advisee about what I have heard.

Sometimes, students like to have a listening party; ask your group if they are interested.

Materials:

A CD for each advisee

Time:

I usually give my advisees a week to complete the CD.

My Life in Music

Have you ever noticed that there seems to be a song for every part of your life? Can you recall major events in your life and immediately think of an associated song? You can probably do this with the good times and the sad times of your life.

Assignment:

Imagine your life as a movie, starting at childhood and moving through your first year out of college. Make a "soundtrack" on the CD I have given you for the movie of Your Life. List the tracks for me so I know what I am listening to, along with the artists' names. Explain why you choose each particular song.

The Rules:

You must have a minimum of seven songs on the CD.

The lyrics have to be "radio edit" or "clean."

You must turn the CD into me by _____

You will get the CD back at the end of the year.

Eyes on the Prize

Values Clarification

Adjustment/Transition/
Role in School

Overview and Suggested Use:

As students move from high school to college and beyond, it is crucial that they begin to separate their own hopes and dreams from those of others. Too often, teenagers' goals have taken shape in the shadow of a parent's goals for them. This exercise helps students clarify what motivates *them* and what *they* want; subsequent exercises will help them lay out how to achieve their goals.

Discussion Prompts/Tips:

Unless the advisee group has been together for some time and is well known to the adviser, this is an exercise that does not lend itself well to discussion. For some students, the answers are too personal and they may be reticent to share with a larger group. If this is the case, an adviser should consider reading the responses and discussing them personally with individual advisees.

Materials:

Pens/pencils

1 copy of the exercise for each student in the group

Advisee folders (Advisee folders are described in the Intro)

Time:

Writing time: 10–12 minutes

Discussion time: variable.

Eyes on the Prize

Answer the following questions (thoughtfully, with more than one-word answers, please!)

Who am I?

What I value most is:

What motivates me is:

What I most like about my school is:

The thing I like least about my school is:

If money, time, and education were not factors, what would you most like to do in your life?

The person I respect most (dead or alive) is:

Why?

Adjustment / Transition / Role in School

Values Clarification

Speak Up!

Character and
Leadership
Development

Values Clarification

Group Dynamics/
Social Development

Health/Life Skills

Overview and Suggested Use:

This is an exercise for older students. I have sometimes used it with leaders such as proctors or captains, and other times with seniors. The goal of the exercise is to help students identify those common implicit cultural assumptions that can be deeply hurtful to classmates, dorm-mates, teammates, etc.

Discussion Prompts/Tips:

This exercise can be difficult to process in a group. I only use it with older students who are also mature, have been together for a long time, and have processed other sensitive exercises together in the past. That said, it is a very good exercise to help students recognize behaviors and challenge norms that are unhealthy or even hurtful.

Materials:

Pens/pencils

1 copy of the exercise for each student in the group

Advisee folders (Advisee folders are described in the Intro)

Time:

Writing time: 10–12 minutes

Discussion time: unlimited

Speak Up!

> *"Courage is what it takes to stand up and speak; courage is also what it takes to sit down and listen."*
> – Winston Churchill

Speak up!

What words are used in the hallways, classrooms, bathrooms, locker rooms, and cafeterias that hurt people?

Are these words used regularly or rarely?

Who uses the words?

Why do you think the people who use the words do so?

What do you think it does to our school?

What does it teach to younger students about our school?

What can you do to stop those words from being used?

What can adults do to stop that language?

How would you ask those adults for assistance in helping you stop hurtful language at our school?

Excellence, According to YOU

Goal Setting

Character and
Leadership
Development

Values Clarification

Academic/Study Skills

Adjustment/Transition/
Role in School

Overview and Suggested Use:

We so often strive for excellence, but we rarely define what excellence means *to us* as individuals, or what actions are required to achieve our version of excellence. High-school aged students are no different. Advisers can help advisees frame their definition of what excellence means *to them* while also encouraging them to think intentionally and deliberately about what actions *they* might take to achieve their version of excellence.

Discussion Prompts/Tips:

The discussion of the question, "What does excellence mean *to you*?" can be a long, energetic conversation because there can be such wide variations amongst the members of the group. Experience has shown that the more lively the discussion, the better the definition of excellence for each individual advisee.

Advisers should be careful that the definitions that advisees use for excellence are not outcome- or materials-based (i.e.: "Owning a huge house and a fleet of Bentleys," or "Being rich") but instead are more values-based (i.e.: "Working as hard as possible at school," or "Leading a large group of supporters"). This is not an easy task, and oftentimes advisers have to send advisees back to the drawing board by asking them to qualify excellence instead of quantifying it.

Materials:

Pens/pencils
1 copy of the exercise for each student in the group
Advisee folders (Advisee folders are described in the Intro)

Time:

Writing time: 10–12 minutes
Discussion time: unlimited.

Excellence, According to YOU

What does excellence mean *to you*?

Where in your life are you making your best effort? List three areas in which you would rate yourself "excellent."

1.

2.

3.

List three areas in which you need to challenge yourself to do—or be—more.

1.

2.

3.

Think of a "badge of excellence," or an outcome goal that you'd like to achieve or have: straight As, start your own business, gain admittance to a top college. List the steps necessary to achieve your goal(s). Write down the name of a person—or an action—to help you with each step.

Most often, the achievement of excellence requires a kind of thinking that is very different from the status quo or the type of thinking of those around you. Where could you use more inventive and creative thinking in order to excel in your schoolwork and your approach to living healthily at school? (i.e.: getting to bed on time, following the rules, etc.)

Continue answers on back of sheet

Adjustment / Transition / Role in School

Academic / Study Skills

Values Clarification

Character and Leadership Development

Goal Setting

Building Competencies

Overview and Suggested Use:

This is an exercise for older, more mature students. I use this exercise most often with 11th graders at the beginning of the school year. It can be difficult for teenagers to understand the definition of "competency" and to recognize the areas in which they possess it, as well as how they can build upon these strengths. When I do this exercise, I try to get my advisees to recognize competencies in others that they lack themselves. This can be challenging for younger students.

Discussion Prompts/Tips:

In my experience, the discussion of this exercise usually centers around two themes: discovering one's own competencies and discovering the competencies of others in the group. I encourage my advisees to use this type of strategic thinking in the future when they work on projects, etc.

Materials:

Pens/pencils

1 copy of the exercise for each student in the group

Advisee folders (Advisee folders are described in the Intro)

Time:

Writing time: 15–20 minutes

Discussion time: unlimited

> *"I have no idols. I admire work, dedication and competence."*
> —Ayrton Senna

Building Competencies

Competency is the ability to do something well, or proficiently. In academics, competencies are things that students should know and be able to do.

What competencies do you think a student needs to reach his or her goals at school?

What competencies do you think a student needs, not only to have knowledge, but also to have goodness? (In other words, what competencies does a student need to do well and to do good?)

How can you develop the competencies you need to achieve your goals?

What are some of the barriers to the development of these competencies; how can you overcome the barriers?

What competencies do you see in other students that compliment your set of competencies? How can you work with these students so that you strengthen each other's weaknesses while also augmenting each other's strengths?

Goal Setting

Values Clarification

Overview and Suggested Use:

Sometimes, to get teens to think about their futures, it helps to encourage them to think beyond themselves in entirely new ways. This exercise inspires teens to think about their futures by considering individuals whom they respect and whose lives they would like to emulate.

I have also had wonderfully deep and thoughtful conversations with advisee groups about the notion of reincarnation and the religions, cultures, and world views that believe in reincarnation—advisers should take a moment and familiarize themselves with the notion of reincarnation if they plan to use this exercise.

Discussion Prompts/Tips:

Teens are usually happy to discuss the first two questions in this exercise with a larger group; they may not always be as open to discussing the final questions. Advisers should gauge the comfort of the group before proceeding to the final questions.

It is crucial for advisers, when using this exercise, to encourage teens to answer the "why" at the end of the first question. Experience has shown that teens are quick to write the name of someone from the sports world (i.e.: "Michael Jordan," "Tom Brady," "Jennifer Rizzotti") or the entertainment world (i.e.: "Jack Johnson," "Tupak," "Charlie Sheen"). Those responses are fine, if they are the result of some deep thinking and consideration, but encourage students to be thoughtful in their responses. I have sometimes used a list of famous inventors, authors, athletes, and politicians to help students broaden their thoughts prior to undertaking the exercise If advisers use this technique, they should take care that the list is a true representation from history, including an international flavor, different races, religions, genders, and sexual orientations.

Materials:

Pens/pencils

1 copy of the exercise for each student in the group

Advisee folders (Advisee folders are described in the Intro)

Time:

Writing time: 10–12 minutes

Discussion time: unlimited.

Trading Places

If you could change lives with any one person, who would it be and why?

What is the one thing you've never had the courage to accomplish?
What would it take to accomplish it?

Relationships and You: What's YOUR Role?

Character and
Leadership
Development

Values Clarification

Group Dynamics/
Social Development

Adjustment/Transition/
Role in School

Health/Life Skills

Overview and Suggested Use:

The etymology of the word relationship is "to carry back." Relationships can be defined as mutual connections, or feelings that exist between two individuals. Each person in a relationship has a responsibility to make that relationship as healthy and as full as it can be. Teens often eschew that responsibility, although usually not intentionally.

I adapted this exercise from one I originally read about in *O* (*The Oprah Magazine*). While her constituents are different, I find that the exercise is quite effective in helping teens understand the nature of relationships, and how they can take responsibility for nurturing connections, new and old.

Discussion Prompts/Tips:

This exercise is for older, more mature students. In my experience, it does not lend itself well to group discussion, especially in all male groups, or groups with mixed gender. However, advisers can meet with individual advisees and discuss their responses to the questions as well as their observations of advisees' relationships at school.

The bonus question can be a difficult one for teens to consider, but it helps to remind them that their relationships today are not temporary or short-lived.

Materials:

Pens/pencils

1 copy of the exercise for each student in the group

Advisee folders (Advisee folders are described in the Intro)

Time:

Writing time: 10–12 minutes

Discussion time: varied—usually individual conversations between adviser and advisee.

"The important thing is not to stop questioning."
–Albert Einstein

Relationships and You: What's YOUR Role?

The etymology of the word relationship is "to carry back." Relationships can be defined as mutual connections, or feelings that exist between two individuals. Each person in a relationship has a responsibility to make that relationship as healthy and as full as it can be. They require much work between all parties. Take a minute and think about a relationship that is special to you—parents, roommate, best friend, coach, teacher, or boyfriend/girlfriend. Answer the following questions about that relationship.

If there was one thing you could change about this relationship, what would it be? Write a step or action you might take to make this change come true.

Poor communication is often the root of problems in relationships. Recall something you said (or didn't say) that you wish you hadn't (or had.) How could you express yourself better in the future if you found yourself in a similar situation? It may be that you need to ask the other person (people) to talk about the situation; how might you start that conversation?

I have often said that relationships are "catalytic" and "enzymatic." In other words, relationships often help us to do something we were unable to do otherwise, but also leave us changed and different. Thinking about this relationship, how have you helped the other person (people) do something that he/she could not have done otherwise and how have you been changed by the relationship (positively or negatively)?

Bonus question: How do you think you will reflect on this relationship in the future?

CHAPTER 3

Spring Forward

Exercises, Assignments, Worksheets for the Spring Semester

As the year progresses, the exercises in this chapter are aimed at helping students continue their work toward grade-appropriate goals. Ninth and tenth grade advisees build on their past successes and continue to improve academically while also working to strengthen connections with peers and adults in the community. Eleventh graders work toward their peak academic performance while also continuing to define who they are for themselves. And twelfth graders, who need to start thinking about living independently at college, are also encouraged to look back on their high school careers and give advice to those in grades behind them .

9TH GRADE

Group Dynamics/
Social Development

Adjustment/Transition/
Role in School

Health/Life Skills

Overview and Suggested Use:

This is a simple and quick exercise to use with younger students who are now familiar with the school and its culture. Just as with adults, teens often befriend other individuals out of a desire to fit in and to have someone to talk with, eat meals with in the cafeteria, etc. As the school year moves toward spring term, friendships will naturally shift and change. This exercise helps advisees deliberately consider those changes and how they can best meet other individuals and get to know them.

Discussion Prompts/Tips:

It is important for advisers to make sure that each advisee has at least one person whom they define as a friend and this exercise accomplishes that. This exercise is an easy way for advisers to check in with advisees about their peer-to-peer relationships.

Materials:

Pens/pencils

1 copy of the exercise for each student in the group

Advisee folders (Advisee folders are described in the Intro)

Time:

Writing time: 10–12 minutes

Discussion time: unlimited.

"The test of courage comes when we are in the minority. The test of tolerance comes when we are in the majority." – Ralph Sockman

People You've Met

Write the name of one person you have met so far at school (adult or student) who has been a positive influence in your life.

How has this person influenced you and why do you consider it to be positive?

How have you positively influenced this person or someone else this term?

What can you do to seek positive, healthy, mature relationships with others in the future?

Character and
Leadership
Development

Group Dynamics/
Social Development

Health/Life Skills

Overview and Suggested Use:

At some point during the first year of high school, students question their ability to do the work, to fit in socially, and whether they have anything in common with their peers. My experience has been that this period of questioning and self-doubt is most acute during the beginning of a new semester. The "newness" of the school and the experience have worn off; the daily schedule has become a routine and a grind. This exercise is aimed at encouraging students to think positively about the many roots they have developed in the school community and to reinforce their place at the school.

Discussion Prompts/Tips:

Embedded in this exercise is one of my favorite questions: "What would you do if you knew you could not fail or be embarrassed?" It is an excellent prompt for discussion with teenagers and it allows them to begin to think about their goals in ways that they might not have before.

Materials:

Pens/pencils

1 copy of the exercise for each student in the group

Advisee folders (Advisee folders are described in the Intro)

Time:

Writing time: 10–12 minutes

Discussion time: unlimited.

"We are all more human than otherwise."
–Harry Stack Sullivan

How I Fit In

Where do you feel you most belong? In other words, where do you feel most comfortable, most at ease, and most like yourself? School, home, church, a team? What strengthens these feelings? What weakens them?

What group do you belong to or activity do you do just for the pure fun of it?

What would you do if you knew you could not fail or be embarrassed?

List six people (living or dead) whom you would like to invite to dinner and why.

Whom do you admire for their ability to bring people together? (Living, dead, related, unrelated.) What qualities stand out in this person? How could you develop these qualities in yourself?

What Type of Student Are YOU?

Overview and Suggested Use:

By this point in the school year, students should have a solid grasp of academic expectations. It has been my experience, however, that students don't always think intentionally and deliberately about how they best achieve and what they wish to achieve. This exercise asks students to be thoughtful about optimizing how they learn and achieve.

Discussion Prompts/Tips:

This exercise is useful because as each student discusses his/her response, other students realize the similarities and differences in how they approach their academic work.

Materials:

Pens/pencils

1 copy of the exercise for each student in the group

Advisee folders (Advisee folders are described in the Intro)

Time:

Writing time: 10–12 minutes

Discussion time: unlimited.

What Type of Student Are YOU?

What words would your current teachers use to describe you?

Describe how you work best. Is it quietly, at a desk, in a group?

What is keeping you from being the best student you can be at school?

What would be one great thing you could accomplish next year? How will you accomplish it?

Adjustment / Transition / Role in School

Academic / Study Skills

Goal Setting

Put a Stake in the Ground!

9TH GRADE

Goal Setting

Values Clarification

Group Dynamics/
Social Development

Overview and Suggested Use:

This is a quick, easy, and fun exercise that I have used effectively with all age groups. I use it in the spring when it is light and warm(er) and nice to be outside. The goal of this exercise is to have students think about what it is they stand for. Each student will literally put a stake in the ground to make their personal declaration.

Discussion Prompts/Tips:

Have each student think about what is important to him/her. For inspiration, sometimes I assemble a slide show of pictures and signs from the Internet: compelling photographs, mottos, political slogans, etc. Have each student write on his or her index card a slogan, a saying, a word, or a picture that they feel represents what they stand for. Staple the index card to the stick and have the students place the stick in the ground outside of the school, their dorm (for boarding students), or their home. If possible, take a picture of all the stakes in the ground to share with the group.

Materials:

Pens/pencils/crayons/markers

3x5 or 5x7 index cards

Sticks (I use chop sticks from a Chinese restaurant)

A strong stapler or tape

Advisee folders (Advisee folders are described in the Intro)

Time:

Writing/drawing time: 10–12 minutes

Discussion time: unlimited—be sure to leave time to put the stakes in the ground!

Character and
Leadership
Development

Values Clarification

Group Dynamics/
Social Development

Health/Life Skills

Overview and Suggested Use:

In January 2003 I was lucky enough to hear Princeton University Professor Cornell West address the students at Phillips Exeter Academy. During his insightful and thoughtful talk, he asked the students why all of the faces depicted on Mt. Rushmore were of white men and asked whom they would put on Mt. Rushmore if it were up to them. This question got me thinking.

This exercise helps students think about who is important to them and why. It also helps students gain and practice vocabulary that enables them to articulate to people who are important to them how they feel.

Discussion Prompts/Tips:

This exercise is easy-to–use and fun, but sometimes, students try to make light of it, suggesting for example, that Mickey Mouse be memorialized on Mt. Rushmore. To help stimulate and broaden their thinking, sometimes I offer students a list of famous inventors, authors, athletes, and politicians before they name their candidates. Remember, if you make a list, take care that the list is a true representation from history, including an international flavor, different races, religions, genders, and sexual orientations.

Many independent schools enroll a number of international students; these students may not fully understand Mt. Rushmore or the figures displayed on the mountain. Advisers should be aware of this and take steps to educate those students in a way that does not embarrass them or make them feel different from the others in the advisee group.

Materials:

Pens/pencils

1 copy of the exercise for each student in the group

Advisee folders (Advisee folders are described in the Intro)

Time:

Writing time: 12–15 minutes

Discussion time: unlimited.

"Good ideas, like good pickles, are crisp, enduring and devilishly hard to make."
—Rushworth M. Kidder

Mount Rushmore

Write the name of four people from history whom you think should be remembered at Mount Rushmore—give specific reasons for your choices.

Write the names of four people from your life who should be memorialized at Mount Rushmore—again, give specific reasons for your choices.

Have you told any of these people how you feel about them? How could you do that?

Picture yourself as being memorialized on Mount Rushmore—what will it take for you to be there?

Healthy Risk Taking

Goal Setting

Character and Leadership Development

Values Clarification

Health/Life Skills

Overview and Suggested Use:

Risk is part of life. Thomas Edison would not have invented the light bulb had he not taken risks; the Internet would not have been possible had Alexander Graham Bell not invented the phone. Risk is something we deal with every day. Usually, we make decisions about risks based on their inherent consequences. Taking healthy risks is something that makes life interesting!

This exercise encourages advisees to define risk in a way they may not have in the past, as a positive thing, and also how to calculate the risk/reward tradeoffs of different actions and decisions.

Discussion Prompts/Tips:

During the discussion of this exercise, advisers need to listen carefully for examples of *healthy* risk taking. Advisers also need to listen carefully for positive and productive risk taking.

Materials:

Pens/pencils

1 copy of the exercise for each student in the group

Advisee folders (Advisee folders are described in the Intro)

Time:

Writing time: 5–7 minutes

Discussion time: unlimited.

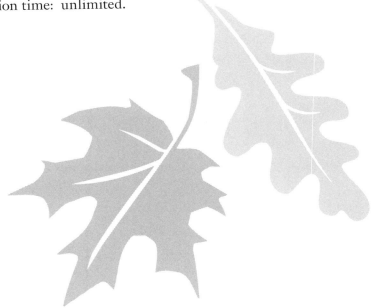

> *"Wisdom is the quality that keeps you from getting into situations where you need it."*
> – Doug Larson

Healthy Risk Taking

Risk is part of life. Thomas Edison would not have invented the light bulb had he not taken risk; the Internet would not have been possible had Alexander Graham Bell not invented the phone. Risk is something we deal with every day. Usually, we make decisions about risks based on their inherent consequences. Taking healthy risks is something that makes life interesting!

Give an example of a healthy risk you have taken. (For example: asked that special someone out to a movie, ordered an extra-spicy taco). What happened? Was the outcome positive or negative? Would you take a similar risk in the future?

What was the decision process you went through in deciding if the risk was worth taking or not? What stops you from taking risks? What are acceptable risks?

For what consequences would you not take a risk?

Wheel of Choices

Character and
Leadership
Development

Values Clarification

Group Dynamics/
Social Development

Health/Life Skills

Overview and Suggested Use:

It is no mistake that my "Wheel of Choices" exercise follows my "Healthy Risk Taking" one. Sometimes, teenagers take risks that are unhealthy. Teens, especially in the age of cell phones and text messaging, often find themselves in situations that they never considered, about which they have no experience, and for which they possess no verbal or emotional vocabulary. This exercise encourages discussion between adults and students about the development of behaviors and actions that students can take when they find themselves faced with rule-breaking behavior.

The overarching message for this exercise is that students "always have a choice" when it comes to their own behavior.

Discussion Prompts/Tips:

This is a simplistic, somewhat tongue-in-cheek approach to encouraging better behavior and the following handout is only a starting place for the discussion. Advisers should encourage, through discussion, and by having advisees develop their own "wheel of choices," and "crisis response" plan.

Materials:

Pens/pencils (if advisers choose to have advisees write their own Wheel of Choices)

1 copy of the exercise for each student in the group and blank sheets of paper if advisers choose to have advisees write their own Wheel of Choices.

Advisee folders (Advisee folders are described in the Intro)

Time:

Writing time (if advisers choose to have advisees write their own Wheel of Choices): 10–12 minutes

Discussion time: unlimited.

"The grace of God is found between the saddle and the ground."
–Irish proverb

Wheel of Choices

You always have a choice!
Use this wheel to help you stay out of trouble and stay away from trouble.

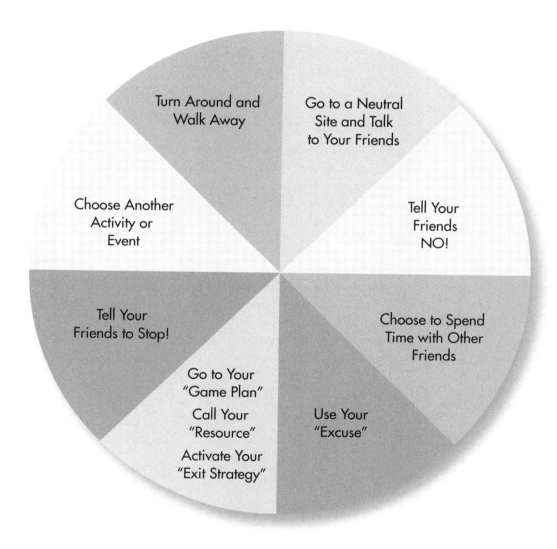

Stay Out of Trouble and Stay Away from Trouble.

Excel: Not Just the Name of a Spreadsheet

Overview and Suggested Use:

Spring semester is usually the right time to ask 10th graders to begin to define "excellence" for themselves, as until now, the concept has often been defined for them by others. As they prepare to enter the home stretch of high school, it is time they differentiate their own definition from those of others.

This exercise also encourages students to think about who can help them attain and sustain excellence, for implicit in these questions is that no one achieves excellence alone.

This exercise comes from one of my colleagues from the Baylor School in Chattanooga, TN, who used it as a writing assignment for proctors (senior student dorm leadership). We have both found it to be very effective.

Discussion Prompts/Tips:

The group discussion around this exercise can be powerful. Usually, when I lead the discussion, as one student explains his or her version of excellence, the others nod and make notes on their paper and add to or change their own version of "excellence."

Materials:

Pens/pencils

1 copy of the exercise for each student in the group

Advisee folders (Advisee folders are described in the Intro)

Time:

Writing time: 10–12 minutes

Discussion time: unlimited.

> *"I do not try to dance better than anyone else. I only try to dance better than myself."*
> – Mikhail Baryshnikov

Excel: Not Just the Name of a Spreadsheet

Inspired by 2002-2003 Baylor School Prefect/Proctor Handbook, used with permission.

What do you need to excel for the remainder of this year and next?

What do you need to excel this week?

Whom will you ask for help?

How will you ask for help?

Who/What are your support systems?

How do you create support systems?

How do you know if you are doing the right thing?

How do you know if you are doing a good job?

Peak Performance

Overview and Suggested Use:

Many times, students have performed at a high level or accomplished something that they had otherwise thought was impossible, or have overcome an obstacle that they once thought insurmountable. Often during those times teens are unaware that they have excelled, and rarely do we allow them the opportunity to reflect on these moments. This exercise asks students to reflect on a time when they achieved a "peak performance" and to focus on which of their actions played a role in that performance so that they might re-create those actions or circumstances in the future.

Discussion Prompts/Tips:

Students generally like to discuss this exercise. It is the adviser's job as moderator to encourage the group to think deliberately and intentionally about what specific steps or actions each member took that led to the peak performances.

Materials:

Pens/pencils

1 copy of the exercise for each student in the group

Advisee folders (Advisee folders are described in the Intro)

Time:

Writing time: 10–12 minutes

Discussion time: unlimited.

Peak Performance

Think of a recent 'peak performance' or an instance where everything seemed to go well, where you felt at ease and comfortable, and the outcome was better than you had hoped. Write down the performance here, its date and time and any other things you remember about it.

Who was there? What was going on around you? What did you do to prepare for the event?

What did you do that had an effect on the positive outcome of this event? Be specific!

What might you do to ensure peak performance in the future? Be specific!

What were the distractions for you, before and during the event? Are these distractions common in your life?

What were you thinking or envisioning in your mind's eye?

What were you saying inside your head and whose voice(s) did you hear?

How did you calm your nerves or get yourself excited for the event?

How do you perform well when you're distracted; how do you minimize distraction prior to an event?

What is the environment you need in order to be successful in the areas you wish to be successful?

Academic / Study Skills

Goal Setting

Telephone Game(s)

Character and
Leadership
Development

Group Dynamics/
Social Development

Overview and Suggested Use:

Too often, issues, concerns, and conflicts arise out of misunderstandings borne of exaggerations and misperceptions. These exercises help demonstrate to students the importance of good communication, and good fact checking in a hands-on, real-world way. Both of the following exercises derive their power from their surprise endings. I try not to repeat them with the same group of students in order to maintain this element of surprise. These exercises take more planning and more time than the others, but the payoffs are huge.

Similar Pictures:

To do the exercise with the pictures below, have the students sit in two side-by-side rows with enough space between the rows that they cannot see each other's drawings. The students should be one behind the other. Review the rules—each student has 45 seconds to replicate the drawing given to him or her by the individual in front of him or her. When 45 seconds are up, the student is to fold his or her drawing over and pass it to the student behind him or her and have that student begin to draw what has just been passed. There should be no talking amongst students during this exercise.

The adviser should collect the drawings as students pass their own back and keep them in order. Walk between the two rows of students and do not allow talking or students to see each other's drawings.

When the student at the end of the row completes his or her drawing, the adviser should hold up the picture, showing the group the similarities between the two original pictures. The adviser should then flip through the drawings the advisees made showing the additions of details that make each of the final pictures different.

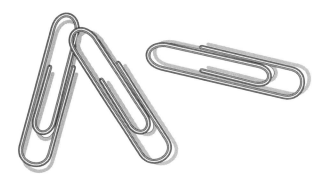

Similar Objects:

To do the 'similar objects' exercise, place pairs of similar objects such as a binder clip and a paper clip inside a paper bag. Pair the students and give one of them the bag. Have them sit back-to-back and allow the student with the bag to put one hand in the bag. After 45 seconds of feeling the objects in the bag, have that student describe to his or her partner what the objects are. The student with the bag is not allowed to use the exact name of the items, but should use other descriptors. For example, a paper clip could be described as "metal and holds papers together." After 45 – 60 seconds of describing the objects, have the individual without the bag guess what the objects are.

The 'brown bag' exercise has many variations; Peter Curran from Blair Academy, shares the version below that adds a leadership twist.

After either exercise is complete, advisers can lead a discussion with students on what it feels like to have to rely on others for primary information, and whether they accepted or questioned that information. Advisers should expand the discussion to include how this type of acceptance—based on others' assumptions and perceptions—occurs in our everyday lives.

Materials:

Pens/pencils

1 copy of the pictures below

Blank pieces of paper

Surfaces on which to write

A place for each student to sit in rows or back-to-back

A stop watch or clock with a second hand

Objects (examples are listed below) and brown paper bags.

Time:

Processing time: 15 - 20 minutes, sometimes longer

Discussion time: unlimited.

Telephone Game(s)

Similar Pictures:

Bomb

Christmas Ornament

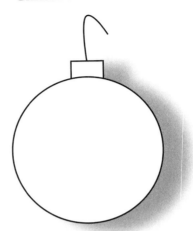

Similar Objects (examples):

Binder Clip—Paper Clip

Pencil—Pen

Quarter—Subway Token

Glue Stick—Chap Stick

Chalk—Dry Erase Marker

Thumb Drive—CD

Lanyard—Key Chain

ID Card—Credit Card

"Brown Bag"

The adviser places one or two dissimilar items from the list below into a brown bag, and hands out one bag to each pair in the group. The group then has about 5 minutes to complete the activity and report out to the others.

Objectives:

The participant will be able to:

- Explain how everyday items can relate to leadership.
- Understand metaphors in leadership.

Activity:

With a partner think of a metaphor for how the items in your brown bag can relate to leadership and list them below:

Eraser:

Paperclip:

Rubber band:

Chocolate hugs:

Granola Bar:

Straw:

Play-Doh:

Goal Setting

Values Clarification

Overview and Suggested Use:

This is a simple activity appropriate for any age or grade level. The exercise encourages students to think about what *they* want for their own future and steps *they* can take to achieve it.

Discussion Prompts/Tips:

Students take to this exercise very quickly. Expect the conversation to be long and boisterous.

Materials:

Crayons or colored markers

1 copy of the exercise for each student in the group

Advisee folders (Advisee folders are described in the Intro)

Time:

Writing time: 10–12 minutes

Discussion time: unlimited.

Snapshot in the Future

Draw a picture of yourself in the box above. Pretend that the picture is taken 15 years in the future. Think about the following: Who are you standing/sitting with? Where are you standing/sitting? What are you standing/sitting in front of? What were you doing just before the picture was taken? What are you going to do right after the picture is taken?

What do you have to do, what steps do you need to take, to make this picture a reality?

Values Clarification

Goal Setting

Easy as Pie

11TH GRADE

Goal Setting

Values Clarification

Academic/Study Skills

Health/Life Skills

Overview and Suggested Use:

This is a common exercise used by educators in many different disciplines—from economics and math to health and leadership classes, and from fourth grade all the way through college. It is a simple, hands-on, self-created demonstration of students' personal strengths and weaknesses. I have used the exercise to help students check the alignment between how they define themselves and how they wish to define themselves.

Discussion Prompts/Tips:

As a follow-up question, ask whether the completed pie chart reflects how advisees *want* to define themselves.

Discussion of this exercise is sometimes best done on an individual basis with advisees. In this case, advisers can compare and contrast with advisees what the student has subjectively written with what the adviser has objectively observed.

Materials:

Pens/pencils/crayons/colored markers

1 copy of the exercise for each student in the group

Advisee folders (Advisee folders are described in the Intro)

Time:

Writing time: 10–12 minutes

Discussion time—unlimited.

Easy as Pie

Divide the circle below into parts (wedges). Each wedge should represent one part of what makes you *you* (i.e: football player, artist, drag racer, etc.). You may have as many wedges as you'd like, however, the size of each wedge should be proportionate to the percentage of what you feel you are.

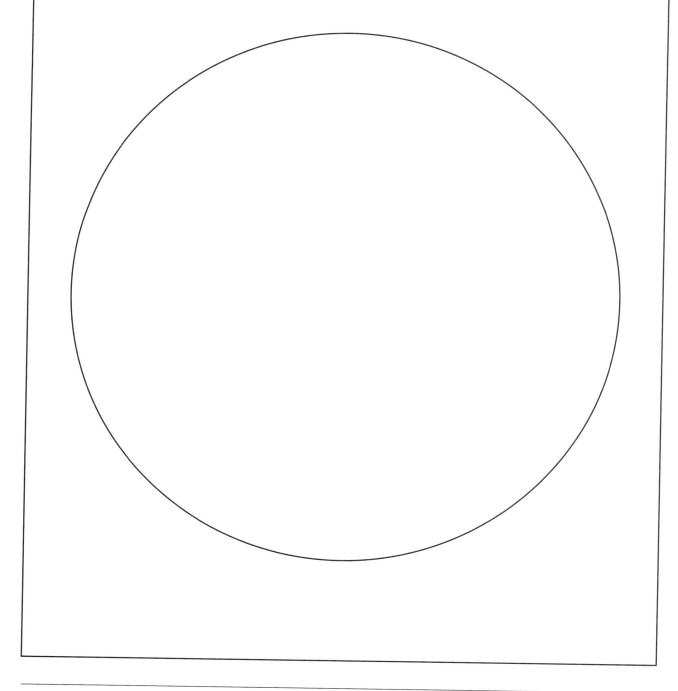

Stress Busters

Values Clarification
Academic/Study Skills
Health/Life Skills

Overview and Suggested Use:

It doesn't take an experienced educator to know that students today feel an enormous amount of stress. Learning how to deal with stress is crucial to academic, emotional, and social success and happiness. This exercise opens up the conversation between students and the adults who care for them about how to effectively recognize and manage stress.

Discussion Prompts/Tips:

Stress is part of life. Stress can be harnessed and put to positive use. Many students struggle just to recognize it! In my experience, the discussion portion of this exercise has generated great sharing within the advisee group on how to best mitigate and manage stress.

For advisee groups, or for individual advisees who report feeling a great deal of stress, I have had them draw a simple picture of their body and indicate where, how, and when they feel or experience the stress.

Students typically respond well to advice on how to best manage stress. My recommendations range from simple suggestions like breathing (seriously, in crisis, people have to be reminded to breathe!) and regular exercise ("minimum volume of vigorous activity"), to proper preparation, organization, visualization, and positive reframing.

Materials:

Pens/pencils—possibly crayons or colored markers

1 copy of the exercise for each student in the group

Advisee folders (Advisee folders are described in the Intro)

Time:

Writing time: 12–15 minutes

Discussion time: unlimited.

"Always laugh when you can."
–Lord Byron

Stress Busters

How do you define stress?

What makes you stressed?

When you are stressed, what do you feel in your body? Be specific: does your stomach churn, does your mouth become dry, do your palms sweat?

What makes you more able to focus on the project, assignment, or task at hand when you are stressed?

What do you think is responsible for your stress?

How do you best manage stress?

How have you heard that other people deal with stress? Have you ever tried their solutions?

Remembering Old Friends While Making New Ones

Values Clarification

Group Dynamics/
Social Development

Overview and Suggested Use:

"Senior Spring" is a time when students become nostalgic about their time in high school and the friendships that have developed there. Advisers should encourage advisees to celebrate these friendships in a healthy way, but also remind students that in college, they'll begin to make new friends. This exercise helps seniors begin to think about the many friends they have, why they call them friends, how those friendships developed, and how they nurtured them.

Discussion Prompts/Tips:

This exercise can be tricky to discuss collectively as some of the students in an advisee group may actually be friends, or the spider web of teenage relationships may extend into the group. In cases where an adviser feels students may have trouble disengaging, or making new friends in college, one-on-one discussions with individual advisees may be more effective.

Materials:

Pens/pencils

1 copy of the exercise for each student in the group

Advisee folders (Advisee folders are described in the Intro)

Time:

Writing time: 10–12 minutes

Discussion time: varied.

Remembering Old Friends While Making New Ones

Friendship was once defined by Noah Webster, and has lately been redefined by Mark Zuckerberg. How do you define "friendship"?

Think for a moment about your friends. Do you have one you consider a "best friend"?

What about that relationship is special?

What was the genesis of that friendship?

Are you someone who makes friends easily? Why or why not?

Are you someone who keeps friendships going easily? Why or why not?

As you move into your senior spring, how can you celebrate the friendships that you do have in a safe and healthy manner?

As you move toward freshman year in college, how do you plan on making new friends in college?

How will you sustain those new friendships, while maintaining the friendships you have now?

Group Dynamics/Social Development

Values Clarification

Goal Setting

Character and
Leadership
Development

Values Clarification

Group Dynamics/
Social Development

Adjustment/Transition/
Role in School

Archway Exercise

Overview and Suggested Use:

I learned a version of this exercise from Kevin O'Neil, the Dean of Studies at Culver Academies, in Culver, Indiana.

Successful students can articulate what they are good for, what they stand for, and what principles guide them. This exercise helps advisees refine their guiding principles in a very concrete manner.

It is crucial for the adviser to make sure that advisees are being very specific in both their choice of words and the definition of those words in order for this exercise to be most effective. Giving the advisee group a list of suggested words one could use to define values is sometimes helpful.

In order to stay on task, advisees should choose four words and only four words.

The actual writing of the words in the spaces should be the final step of this exercise, and the writing should be in pen to signify permanence.

Discussion Prompts/Tips:

As advisees choose words, ask them to define them for one another—this will help them be specific in their choices.

Sometimes I use this exercise at the beginning of the school year, and have my advisees post their four words on paper above my office (classroom) door, or, over the door to their rooms (for boarding students).

I often use this exercise with leadership groups, and at the end of the discussion ask them what steps/actions they can take if the words in the archway do not reflect reality. I also ask them to identify adult allies to help them with those steps and actions.

Materials:

Pens/pencils
1 copy of the exercise for each student in the group
Advisee folders (Advisee folders are described in the Intro)

Time:

Writing time: 15 – 20 minutes
Discussion time: unlimited.

Archway Exercise

Picture an archway or an entry way into your house, room, homeroom, or dorm. Above the archway are written four words. The words are there because they describe the qualities and principles for which the people who live there stand. Think for a moment about what you'd like the words in your archway to be; write them in the spaces provided below.

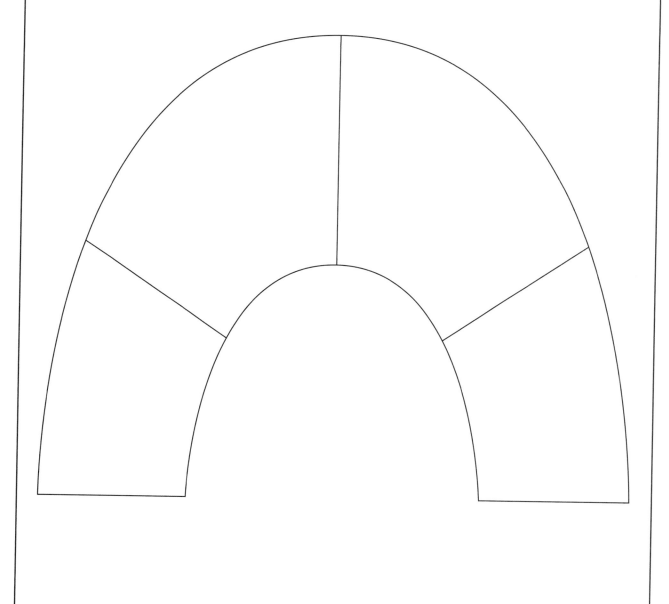

Adjustment/Transition/Role in School

Group Dynamics/Social Development

Values Clarification

Character and Leadership Development

Goal Setting

How Do I Want to Start College?

12TH GRADE

Goal Setting

Values Clarification

Academic/Study Skills

Adjustment/Transition/
Role in School

Health/Life Skills

Overview and Suggested Use:

For many high school seniors, the quest for college acceptance is a grueling obsession that eclipses the realization that they will actually be attending college.

Colleges and universities have recognized for years that the more thoughtful and mentally prepared for college one is, the better the outcome that 'first year' will be. Advisers can help advisees prepare for their college experience by having them think, write, and talk about some of the potential pitfalls and challenges, that if not properly handled, can mar that all-important first year.

Discussion Prompts/Tips:

This exercise can be challenging for seniors to tackle and even trickier to discuss; which is all the more reason it is so useful. It forces seniors to consider the many milestones and challenges that can attend the first few months of school.

Materials:

Pens/pencils

1 copy of the exercise for each student in the group

Advisee folders (Advisee folders are described in the Intro)

Time:

Writing time: 15–20 minutes

Discussion time: varies, usually not long

"Pick your battles."
–Leo Morrissey

How Do I Want to Start College?

The term "making friends" accurately describes the process of meeting new people. "Make" is an action verb and meeting new people requires work to get to know people while we let others learn about us. Any faculty member will tell you that the friends that you make in the first four weeks at a new school may not be the friends that you will necessarily have by the final four weeks. Friendships evolve and change over the years. Think about the friends you have now and ask yourself:

How did I make those friendships? What did I do to nurture those friendships?

One of the best ways for you to "make" friends is to get involved in school activities. What are some activities you would like to continue to be involved with at college? What are some new activities you would like to try?

If you have a boyfriend or girlfriend, have you discussed with him or her how you will stay in touch and what level of commitment you expect from each other?

Some things to think about when you head off to college:

- It is difficult to make friends at college if you are on the cell phone with your friends from high school. Cell phones and social networking sites are a real challenge to overcoming homesickness. Like many tools, cell phones and computer screens do have a downside when viewed in the light of students new to a community who are trying to transition smoothly into that new environment. One of the things that makes the education at college so rich and complete is the opportunity for students to develop independence and self-reliance. Students, who have in the past had feelings associated with homesickness, should minimize long, drawn out cell phone conversations with folks from home. This may seem counterintuitive; however, experience shows that students who get out, meet new people, and try new things will transition more rapidly than those who spend time on the phone with friends and family at home or another school.

- Spend some time when you first get to college researching whom you can call or go to when you need help. Potential useful resources include: the campus safety office, counseling center, academic support center, and residential life office. In each instance, make note of the facility's location and contacts.

- For many freshmen, college is their first time they share a room or live with someone who is not a family member. Living with people who are different from us is an important life skill and crucial to success in college. Students with roommates should sit down with them ahead of time and discuss key issues such as housekeeping, bedtimes, study sessions, and the sharing and respecting of personal property.

Continue answers on back of sheet

Words of Wisdom

Values Clarification

Group Dynamics/
Social Development

Adjustment/Transition/
Role in School

Health/Life Skills

Overview and Suggested Use:

This exercise is fun and easy-to-use with students in their final year/semester of high school. It is a great way for advisers to learn more about what students feel they need.

Discussion Prompts/Tips:

Sometimes I give this exercise to my advisees prior to our group meeting in order to give them time to think about their responses. I always tell my advisees that I also welcome their suggestions for advice to younger students any time.

Materials:

Pens/pencils

1 copy of the exercise for each student in the group

Advisee folders (Advisee folders are described in the Intro)

Time:

Writing time: 12 - 15 minutes

Discussion time: unlimited.

> *"Follow in my wake, there's not that much at stake, for we have plowed the seas and smoothed the troubled waters…"* – Jimmy Buffet

Words of Wisdom

What advice did you receive before coming to school here?

What advice did you not receive, but wish you had?

What advice would you tell an adviser to give new students (prior to coming to school, early in the year, or at any time during the year)?

Personal Mission Statement

Overview and Suggested Use:

Writing a personal mission statement is the culmination of the advising curriculum. This exercise brings together elements from four years. Prior to working on writing a mission statement, advisers should have advisees review their advisee folder (described in the Intro) and pay particular attention to the following exercises: "What Do You Bring to the Team?," "30 Second Commercial," "Short Bios," "Easy as Pie," and "Archway Exercise."

Mission statements are best when concise. Every word should count with nothing extra to get in the way or weaken the way students choose to describe themselves. Effective mission statements are documents that guide students through life's many choices and help them focus on what is important to them, and what they want to accomplish. Remind students that the best mission statements are ones that are reviewed and updated regularly.

Discussion Prompts/Tips:

No question, this exercise is challenging. Many students will struggle to write a concise, powerful mission statement. Be sure that students keep their mission statements positive and talk about what they do, and do well, rather than what they do not do, or do not want to do. Some students need a template to get started. Ask students to write what they want to do—as though they were applying for a job—and to begin each question with the phrase, "To be…" Another method is to have each student begin each statement with, "I am…" The latter method allows students to more easily add values to their statements, using terms such as "charity," "compassion," "integrity," etc. Also, some students are more easily able to come up with a mission statement if the last line starts with, "And I will…" following by a stated goal for their lives.

It sometimes takes two or three sessions to polish a personal mission statement.

Materials:

Pens/pencils

1 copy of the exercise for each student in the group

Advisee folders (Advisee folders are described in the Intro)

Time:

Writing time: varies

Discussion time: varies

"Put the heart before the course."
–H.H. Bissell

Personal Mission Statement

Write down two or three things you are passionate about—a sport, a musical instrument, art, family, community service. Be specific—if you are passionate about a playing a musical instruments, say "guitar," not "music."

Write down three things that you are good at, especially things at which you feel you are better than others. Write a few words explaining why you think you are good at these things, for example: "I am good at math because I see solutions to problems differently than others."

Write a few words you would use to describe yourself.

Write down a few words others use to describe you.

Knit the above into a statement that is three to five sentences long that
1. Describes you (I am…) and what you want to accomplishment in your life; (And I will…); and
2. Describes how you will accomplish it (By doing…)

Adjustment / Transition /
Role in School

Academic / Study Skills

Group Dynamics/Social
Development

Values Clarification

Character and Leadership
Development

Goal Setting

CHAPTER 4

Goal Setting Exercises

As I stated in the Introduction of this workbook, there is no more valuable lesson an adviser can teach advisees than how to set goals. The exercises and instructions in this chapter help advisers get advisees to focus on precisely this task, beginning with "Goal Refresher" at the start of the term, and moving through to "End-of-Term Goal Setting" exercises. There are variations on the same theme to allow advisers to try multiple approaches to this all-important project.

Goal Refresher

Overview and Suggested Use:

As I stated earlier, setting goals is a crucial step in helping high school students achieve a desired outcome. This is a simple and quick exercise best used at the beginning of the term, to remind students what they are working toward and why and how they have chosen to focus on their goals.

Discussion Prompts/Tips:

This exercise can be completed very quickly by students, both new and returning. Advisers can even send this exercise to advisees to be completed by email.

Materials:

Pens/pencils or email address

1 copy of the exercise for each student in the group—or 1 copy sent via email

Advisee folders (Advisee folders are described in the Intro)

Time:

Writing time: 5–7 minutes

Discussion time: discussions of goals are best done individually.

Goal Refresher

Take a moment and think back to last semester.

I asked you to set goals for the term, for the year, and for the next three years. I also asked you to write down some steps on how you would achieve each goal, as well as the names of a few peers and adults who could help you to achieve those goals. Now think about those goals and those steps. Reminder: the goals I encouraged you to set were not "outcome" or "achievement" goals like "getting all As," "making the varsity team," or "becoming Student Council President," but were instead process-based goals that would allow you to achieve the best possible outcome. Examples of process goals include: "I will study for two hours each night without a computer on in my study space," "I will practice my sport for an hour a day and lift weights and run three times per week," or "I will attend Student Council meetings each week and vote according to how I feel about the issues, not how my friends tell me to vote."

Remind yourself of those goals and make sure that they are still the goals you want for yourself.

It is time to take the steps you outlined as necessary to achieve your goals.

It is time to enlist the assistance of your peers and the adults whom you identified as individuals who could help you achieve those goals.

Midterm Goals Review

Overview and Suggested Use:

Every school has some type of feedback for students around the midterm point. Usually, this midterm feedback is given in terms of a letter grade or number grade in each class. It has been my experience that most schools do not require written teacher comments, or student-teacher meetings at the midterm point, so all students have to gauge their progress on is a letter or a number grade. How that grade was calculated, whether class participation, lab results, homework grades, etc. were included varies from teacher to teacher, department to department, and school to school.

Rarely is there feedback from co-curricular or extracurricular activities such as student clubs or organizations and teams.

This exercise encourages students to reflect on the term and then either update their goals accordingly, or change their effort or actions so that they are more on track to achieve their stated goals.

Discussion Prompts/Tips:

No experienced educator needs to be reminded that students (and their parents!) are very achievement and outcome focused (did someone say grades?). It is important to continually reframe advisees' thinking, so that they concentrate more on process and task and less on actual results.

Materials:

Pens/pencils

1 copy of the exercise for each student in the group

Sheets of paper for each student

1 envelope for each student

Advisee folders (Advisee folders are described in the Intro)

Time:

Writing time: 12–15 minutes

Discussion time: discussions of goals are best done individually.

> *"Achievable goals are the first step to self-improvement."*
> –J. K. Rowling

Midterm Goals Review

Here is your assignment:

Step One:

- Review the goals you set for yourself at the end of the last term. (The most recent set is located in your Advisee Folder in a signed and dated envelope.)

- Think about your most recent feedback from classes. Does this feedback reflect your effort and focus in each class? Would you consider the feedback to indicate achievement of your goals?

- Think about other activities at school—student clubs, drama production, athletics, community service. Have you received feedback (implicit or explicit) from anyone in those areas? Does this feedback reflect your effort and focus in each class? Would you consider the feedback to be achievement of your goals?

- If you did not get it, could you seek explicit feedback from leaders in those areas? How would you go about this?

Step Two:

- What has gone well at school thus far?

- What has not gone so well?

- What actions have I taken this term that might have helped me achieve the goals, and with which I am pleased.?

- What actions have I taken or not taken this term that might have helped me achieve the goals, and with which I am not pleased?

Step Three:

- Write a goal you have for the rest of the term.

- Write a goal you have for the year.

- Write a goal you have for the next three years.

- Along with the goals write a few strategies (be specific!) that might help you achieve these goals.

Place them in the envelope, sign and date the seal, and pass in to me.

Please don't hesitate to see me with any question, comments, or problems. I am available to talk about your goals—please let me know if you would like to!

Good luck, I hope this exercise helps.

End-of-Term Goal Setting I and II

Overview and Suggested Use:

As I have mentioned earlier, there is a preponderance of data suggesting that setting goals for oneself helps in the achievement of those goals. It is crucial that teens set *their own* goals, separate from their parents and their peers.

This exercise assists students in setting goals for themselves, and documenting them so they can review and build upon them.

Discussion Prompts/Tips:

Remind students that their goals should be process-oriented and not achievement- or results-oriented.

Materials:

Pens/pencils

1 copy of the exercise for each student in the group

Sheets of paper for each student

1 envelope for each student

Advisee folders (Advisee folders are described in the Intro)

Time:

These exercises specify the amount of time that each advisee should spend on them.

Discussion time: discussions of goals are best done individually.

End-of-Term Goals 1

This is your end-of-the-term "assignment." It is aimed at helping *you* improve your approach to both academics and stressors you might encounter. I hope that by accepting it in the spirit it is offered, you will thrive in the upcoming semester and beyond.

Step One:

Find a quiet place where you will be comfortable and undisturbed for at least 30 minutes.

Step Two:

- Reflect on the past semester: (**read through the folder I have returned to you!**)
- What went well?
- What actions of yours resulted in things going well?
- What else contributed to your success?
- What did not go as well as you wished or expected?
- What actions (or inactions) resulted in things not going well?
- What else contributed to things not going as you had planned?
- Think of a time during the term when you were upset, sad, or stressed.
- What were the precipitating factors?
- What helped you to deal with the hard time?
- If nothing helped, why didn't anything help?
- Think of one thing you do really well.
- Why or how do you have a proficiency in this area?
- How could you apply attaining this expertise to other areas in your life?
- Think of one thing you don't do well.
- Why or how do you lack expertise in this area?
- How does this lack of proficiency extend into other areas of your life?

Continued next page

End-of-Term Goals I (continued)

Step Three:

You need to somehow put the thoughts on the above on paper. *(This exercise only becomes effective with this step!)* You can do this any way that works *for you*. You could: write a letter to yourself, write the lyrics to a song, write the music to a song, draw or paint a picture, write a poem, draw a "mind map," choreograph a dance, etc.

Step Four:

- Write a goal you have for the next term.
- Write a goal you have for the year.
- Write a goal you have for the next three years.
- Along with the goals, write a few strategies *(be specific!)* that will help you achieve these goals.
- Also, write down a few strategies that might help you improve some of the weaknesses you discovered during your reflection (Step Two).

Write the names of adults in the community who could help you stay on the path to achieve your goals.

Write all of the above (Step Four) on the paper provided.

Please don't hesitate to ask any questions!

End-of-Term Goals II

It's that time again!

Read your grades and comments.

Read the "goals" you wrote from the end of fall term. That was a long time ago.

Step One:

- Write a goal you have for the next term.
- Write a goal you have for the year.
- Write a goal you have for the next three years.
- Along with the goals, write a few strategies (be specific!) that might help you achieve these goals.
- Also, write down a few strategies that might help you improve some of the weaknesses you discovered during your reflection (Step Two).
- Write the names of adults in the community who could help you stay on the path to achieving your goals.

Step Two:

- Think about the following questions:
- Did I reach the goals I set for myself?
- Why or Why not? (Be specific!)

Step Three:

- Ask yourself the following questions:
- What are my strengths?
- How can I use my strengths to reach my goals?
- What are my weaknesses?
- How can I improve on my weaknesses so that they do not become an obstacle for me in reaching my goals?

Step Four:

- Write a goal you have for the next term.
- Write a goal you have for the year.
- Write a goal you have for the next three years.
- Along with the goals, write a few strategies (be specific!) that might help you achieve these goals.

Place them in the envelope, sign and date the seal, and put them into your advisee folder.

Goal Rubric

Overview and Suggested Use:

This exercise was given to me by my friend Pete Curran, Dean of Student Life at Blair Academy, in Blairstown, NJ. Although he is not sure of its origin, he reports that this exercise has floated around Blair for some time and is widely used by advisers with great success.

I like the exercise because, unlike most of the goal-setting exercises I use, it forces students to share their goals graphically. For some students, this format is easier to grasp and understand. I also like that, at Blair, they have encouraged advisers to place an emphasis on the "effort" grade.

Discussion Prompts/Tips:

Remind students that their goals should be process-oriented and not achievement- or results-oriented.

Materials:

Pens/pencils

1 copy of the exercise for each student in the group

1 envelope for each student

Advisee folders (Advisee folders are described in the Intro)

Time:

15–20 Minutes

Discussion time: discussions of goals are best done individually.

Class	Mid Semester Grades		1st Semester Goal		Steps necessary to achieve goals
	Academic Mark	Effort Mark	Academic Mark	Effort Mark	
					1. 2.
					1. 2.
					1. 2.
					1. 2.
					1. 2.
					1. 2.
					1. 2.

Name:

Date:

CHAPTER 5

Effectively Communicating with Advisee Parents

Effective advisers intentionally, deliberately, and regularly communicate with the parents of advisees. While I have come to liken advising to "objective parenting," there is no substitute for well-organized communication with the "subjective" parties in the equation, namely the parents who have entrusted their precious offspring to the school's care. To this end, this chapter contains best practices on those communications, including advice on managing parent meetings and ready-to-use templates for correspondence.

From In Loco Parentis to Societas Parentis

In Loco Parentis is a legal term that means "in place of a parent" or "instead of a parent." (It does not mean, as many colleagues have tried to convince me over the years, "in with crazy parents.") The term indicates that an individual, institution, or organization takes on some of the responsibilities of a parent for a minor. The term suggests that the individual, institution, or organization would act, just as a parent would, in the best interest of the student.

Societas Parentis is my own term; I use it to mean "in partnership" with parents, "in league" with parents, or "in association" with parents. It has been my experience that when they think of parents as partners, advisers are more easily able to communicate with them on a variety of topics and issues. And vice versa: things also go more smoothly when parents feel that they are in a partnership with an adult at the school, and that they have an ally who can guide them through the school's systems and bureaucracy.

Partnering with parents requires deliberate, intentional, regular, careful, and patient communication via a variety of media—meetings, email, Web, and phone. It takes real effort, in other words.

Field Notes

Creating Societas Parentis from a Veteran Adviser / Teacher / Coach / Dean / Dorm Head:

Parents are "Post-Columbine," Post-9/11," "Post-Virginia Tech," and many are apprehensive about dropping their son or daughter off at school.

My father recounts for me the drills he went through as a student during the Cold War where he would have to hide beneath his desk and then shuffle to the "fallout" shelter. Today we are privy to (or is it victimized by?) a different sort of threat: a constant stream of information, 24 hours a day, 7 days a week. Much of it is frightening and not very positive. Raising a child in the 21st century is an exhilarating, but fraught, adventure, and it takes time for parents to trust that school is a safe and supportive place for their child.

Parents are nervous about college.

College applications continue to rise and admissions continue to become more selective; at the same time, tuition grows seemingly exponentially. Parents are anxious about the college process and about college admissions; they have invested hundreds of thousands of dollars into their own hopes and dreams for their sons and daughters. It can be difficult (sometimes impossible!) for parents to understand when their son's and daughter's hopes and aspirations diverge from theirs. It is also painful when a son's or daughter's hopes and aspirations about a college don't pan out; it will likely be, for most parents, the first time that they were unable to positively affect an outcome for their child.

Parents are as cell phone, text message, IM, and social network savvy as you are (they have already "Googled" you, and are now looking at your Facebook page).

Parents use the same methods of communications that you and students use. Advisers can put this to their advantage by setting up Facebook pages, or by Tweeting updates for the group. Remember to check with your school's communications department for its acceptable social media use policy ahead of time.

Many parents are accustomed to regular, quantitative feedback (sometimes daily and sometimes as reported by their son or daughter).

Most lower and middle schools keep online grade books and homework calendars, and many upper schools and high schools do not. For parents who are used to daily feedback and are accustomed to having to sign homework notebooks, high school can be a very foreign place. To rely on their son's or daughter's reports on their own progress can be challenging or unsettling for parents, especially when the progress reports may not be accurate.

Sons and daughters have always been the ones that everyone else has turned to for help and now need to ask for help.

For many students, entering high school is academically challenging; add in emotional and social developments, and young students can find themselves adrift at sea. For many, this is the first time that they might need to ask for help, something completely foreign to them which may cause feelings of shame and embarrassment.

Whatever you say will be repeated, from the teen perspective.

Never expect confidentiality or privacy from a teenager—they will always repeat what you say, and repeat it from their own perspective, which will not be complimentary. Use caution when speaking with students; do not share secrets or stories or use language that is inappropriate. If you err, own it, apologize for it, and learn from the experience.

Get your message "out there" before they do.

There will be times, probably many, when you will need to deliver bad news, reprimand a student, or otherwise say or do the right thing, and the student will be unhappy about it. In these instances, if it is logistically possible, it is better to prepare communication to the parent and have it ready to go just after delivering the news, or the decision. Again, your decision, actions, and words will be delivered to the parent in a manner that sheds the best light on the student and the worst possible light on the adviser, and may not be in any way factual. Be prepared to reframe the facts as presented to the parent while at the same time being careful not to call the student a liar. Some handy suggested phrases include:

"I'm surprised she took that away from our conversation…," "I fear that I may have been misquoted…," and "Let me tell you the back story your daughter may have forgotten to mention…"

Don't make promises you can't keep.

If I had a nickel for every time a parent called me and asked me not to tell their son or daughter that they were calling, I would not be writing this book; I would be relaxing with my millions on a beach somewhere! In fact, early on during my adviser/advisee relationship, I tell parents that if they don't want their son or daughter to know that they called, emailed, or met with me, they should not call, email, or meet with me.

Know your school's graduation requirements, or know someone who does.

As an adviser, you must know what credits from which subject areas each student needs to graduate. If you are new to the school or do not work in an academic department, find an individual who knows the requirements and meet with him or her regularly to make sure each of your advisees is on track for graduation.

Know the rhythm of the school year.

As I mentioned in Chapter 1, every school has a rhythm to the academic year—there is an amplitude and frequency to the pace of life, and the workload and the daily/weekly schedule. Knowing this rhythm and communicating with advisees and their parents accordingly, will help them navigate the school more smoothly and also more successfully. I encourage advisers to use a calendar to map out the entire school year in order to be proactive with communication to parents and advisees.

It is crucial that advisers know the schedule for special weekends such as Parents' Weekend and Grandparents' Weekend, and make themselves available (as schedules allow) for parent meetings.

It is better to say, "I don't know," than to give an incorrect response.

Many parents will call, email, or visit you expecting an immediate response. It is always acceptable (and prudent!) to slow down the process and to find the correct answers to questions. Tell parents that you are not sure of a practice or policy but that you will check on it and get back to them.

Advisers at boarding schools should remember that you are visiting the students in their bedrooms.

When visiting a student in his or her room, be sure to keep the light(s) on, keep the door slightly ajar, dress appropriately, and never sit on the bed.

Remind parents that being uncomfortable is not the same as being unhappy.

Students will call parents about challenges they face, issues that upset them, and answers they receive from adults at school with which they disagree. Parents will quickly try to intervene on their child's behalf to get for them what they perceive their student wants or needs. Remind parents that your school is academically rigorous, and that its policies, procedures, and practices are designed to 1) keep students safe, 2) maintain a culture of academic rigor and integrity, and 3) be fair to the entire community. That their teen is uncomfortable does not mean that he or she is unhappy.

Set goals for each message, phone call, or meeting.

In order for communication to be effective and well received, it should be clear and concise. Keep messages and meetings short; let your advisee know what your messages are and what happened during a parent meeting. Including advisees in the planning of meetings is a very useful strategy. Prior to a phone call, write a few talking points so that you can keep on point.

Never ever worry alone.

If you ever have a concern about a student, share it with an administrator, a department chair, a counselor, or the school nurse. Seek advice from experienced advisers!

Document, document, document!

When you have a conversation with a student or a parent, take a moment to jot a note or two about what was said, what conclusions were made, what actions steps were outlined, or what instructions you gave the student. The note need not be extensive, but should be legible and easy to retrieve if needed.

Preparing Parents for the "Dump Call"

There is a phenomenon that affects almost every parent of a high-school aged student. The phenomenon occurs when a boarding student calls his or her parents and complains about the school, complains about the teachers, the dorm, the food, the coaches, and the town in which the school is located, etc. Day students do the very same thing, except that they go home one night and download on their parents, usually just as the parent is about to go to bed.

My good friend, Matt Radtke, the Director of Admissions at the Hammond School in Columbia, SC, and I termed this phenomenon, "The Dump Call." After the student "dumps" all of his or her frustrations on the parent, he or she feels immediately and markedly better— and the parents fall into a state of panic and despair. Panic and despair combine with an utter hopelessness as they really don't know what to do. After all, like all proper 21st-century parents, we are programmed to fix any and all of our son's or daughter's problems.

The Dump Call is not really about a single problem, issue, or concern at school. If there is a specific issue, problem, or concern, the vast majority of students will be able to articulate it, specifically. Instead, the Dump Call is about frustration, workload, a feeling of aloneness, exhaustion, fear of failure, hormones, and teen angst. It is crucial that someone at your school warn parents of new students about the Dump Call during orientation, and it is vital that advisers recognize the Dump Call when parents report it. One never wants to minimize the call, or suggest that there isn't reason for it—but usually, the reasons for the call are varied and nebulous, and resolution is often a matter of simply speaking with the student, reassuring him or her, and reminding him or her of the support systems in place at the school. It is never a bad idea to alert the school counselor that a parent has reported a Dump Call to you, and when I hear of one happening with an advisee, I usually follow up personally with him/her as soon as is feasible. I follow up again two days later and then a week later, each time also calling, emailing, or meeting with the student's parents.

Meet the Parents: Some Winning Strategies

At some point during the school year, each adviser is going to have to meet with a certain number of advisee parents. I use the term "meeting" loosely, to include not only face-to-face, sit-down encounters, but increasingly, phone calls or Skype conversations, as well. Whatever the format, advisers should be prepared for their occurrence both during the regular school year calendar, as well as during special events like Parents' Weekend. Sometimes parent-adviser meetings are the result of a concern about an individual advisee's academic performance, social or emotional adjustment to school, or behavior. Whatever the reason for the meeting(s), it is crucial that advisers be prepared for them and work to make them as successful as possible for all parties—parents, adviser, and advisee.

No one will ever know an advisee better than his or her parents, but at the same time parents expect that advisees will know their son or daughter as well as or better than anyone at school. As such, when preparing for an adviser-parent meeting, I review as much information as I can beforehand, and have at my fingertips any relevant material. I review advisee grades, course comments, and transcripts. If the meeting is regarding an advisee's behavior, I review the student handbook and the parent handbook ahead of time, and have a copy of both handy.

When possible, I have my advisees attend parent-adviser meetings. I also prefer that advisees take the lead in these meetings, and typically prepare them to lead by giving them some structure with the following questions:

- What do you want to accomplish during the meeting? (This is actually a question I ask advisee parents and myself, as well.)

- Examples of advisee responses include: "I want my parents to know how hard the academics are here and that I am doing my best to reach my potential." "I want to let my parents know that it has been really hard to transition here and that has negatively affected my grades." "I want to show my parents that I am not a math/science person, that my passion is theater."

- How will you know if you have achieved your goals for the meeting?

- What do *you* want to share with your parents during the meeting?

- What do you want to *me* to share with your parents during the meeting?

- Is there something you prefer I not share at the meeting and why? (I do tell my advisees that there are some things that I must share, and if that is the case, we work out a script for me so that the advisee has control over sensitive subjects and issues.)

- What data/evidence/support/back-up do you need to bring to the meeting? Will your advisee need a computer or other A/V setup for the meeting?

- How can I (as your adviser) help you during this meeting?

- What would you like from your parents after the meeting?

- What would you like from me (as your adviser) after the meeting?

- What do you need to do after the meeting?

- What kind of follow up should there be after the meeting?

Writing Effective, Complete, and Useful Adviser Comments that Help Advisees Achieve their Goals

Most schools have a system in which advisers write some number of reports or "comments" that become part of the student's record and that are made available to parents. Usually, comments are completed between two and four times a year, and usually after a grading period.

Writing effective comments is another way in which advisers can assist their advisees in achieving their personal goals. I break advisee comments into five areas. (My brother is a professor of English Literature at Clemson University—he loathes the five paragraph essay, so my apologies to him!) I have a folder on my desk where I keep a running list of notes about my advisees; when it is time to write the comments, I pull out the notes and knit them into sentences, paragraphs, and a full, complete comment. Peter Curran, the Dean of Student Life at Blair Academy, has shared with me a questionnaire that he has used at both Blair and Fountain Valley School, in Colorado; he then adds to the questionnaire a set of very specific instructions for advisers to follow. Both are included below, but I draw your attention to the last question: "Is there anything additional you'd like me to add to my Adviser Letter?"

My five-paragraph approach:

- I review for parents the activities that both my advisee and my advisee group have been involved in since the last time I wrote a comment. I add to the comment a brief review of any goal setting exercises that the group has done and invite parents to discuss the exercises with their son or daughter.

- I review the activities in which my advisee has been involved since the last time I wrote— activities such as sports, extra-curricular pursuits, community services, etc.

- I review any observations I have made regarding my advisee's social life at school—the size of his/her group of friends, the breadth of the types of friends, what their activities and hobbies appear to be.

- I review any observations that I have made or heard from individual teachers about my advisee's efforts.

- I review the comments my advisee's teachers have made about his/her performance in class.

- I try to conclude (maybe that's a sixth paragraph!) by highlighting any suggestions for improvements individual teachers have made for advisees in their individual classes.

The "Adviser Comment Sheet" as used at Blair Academy & Fountain Valley School

Three things I have done this semester that I am proud of:

Overall, this semester has been:

My greatest academic success this semester has been:

What I did to make this happen:

As the end of the semester approaches I worry about:

 Why:

 What I am willing to do to make this better:

This semester my sport experience has been:

This semester I tried something new/exciting/challenging:

My favorite extracurricular activities are:

My social life is:

*For Boarders only - Life in my Res Hall has been:

*For Day Students only - Something I could use help with is:

What, if anything, would you like to change about your daily routine, weekend habits, friendships, or relationships with teachers, coaches, and dorm parents?

I need my Adviser to:

Anything additional you'd like me to add to my Adviser Letter?

Adviser Letter Template from Blair Academy and Fountain Valley School

When writing an adviser letter, always make sure to have specific information to share with parents. These letters are not nearly as significant if they include general statements—parents pay a lot of money to send their children to your institution, and they are expecting that you not only know their children, but that you can write confidently and succinctly about their life at your school.

Also, make sure that one of your colleagues proofreads your letters before they go into the mail. Whether your school has set up a formal proofreading process or you informally exchange your letters with a colleague, make sure a second set of eyes reads your writing.

Finally, be aware if your advisee has a sibling who attends your school. If your advisee has a sibling, then the parents will receive two sets of adviser letters. All of your advisee letters should be thoughtful and full of rich details, but especially with siblings, make sure that the information is thorough; parents will compare and you would be embarrassed if your letter were vastly different (i.e. inferior) than your colleague's.

The quality of your letter is a direct reflection on you as an adviser and on your institution; well written, thorough, and informative letters provide a tremendous service in terms of maintaining lines of communication between us and parents. Poorly written letters do us all a disservice. Topics to include in your adviser letter:

- Adjustment to school life
- Attitude
- Citizenship and conduct
- Performance in academic, extracurricular activities, and athletics
- Life in the residential hall
- Goals
- Challenges and rewards

Remember

1. You are expected to have a broad overview of the student, but make sure to include specific statements. Anecdotes can be very helpful in giving letters a personal touch.

2. Make sure your salutation is correct.

3. Before writing your letter, it can be helpful to reread the student's admissions questionnaire and the new parent questionnaire if your advisee is a new student.

4. If you have a comment sheet/questionnaire that you discuss with your advisees before writing your letter, feel free to use this information in your letter.

5. Ask your advisees if there is anything they would like you to include in your letter; sometimes they will give you a humorous line or some valuable information that they would like you to share with their parents (obviously you need to decide if the information is appropriate before including it in your letter).

6. Feel free to include a brief paragraph near the beginning (perhaps as the introduction) about the other students in your adviser group and some of the activities that you do together during adviser period.

Ready-to-Use Examples of Adviser-Parent Communication
(sample email)

Greeting and reminder—sent about two weeks into the school year:

Hello! My name is _____; I am the Dean of Students. I am writing to remind you that I have been assigned to be your son's or daughter's adviser while at school.

The adviser is the individual on campus who oversees a student's social, emotional, and academic transition and success at school. We are the primary contact at school for parents.

You should feel free to contact me via email or phone. My cell phone is _____, my number at school is _____.

Enjoy the last few weeks of fall!

Note about the rhythm of the school:

Hello Families!

A few weeks have passed since I last wrote and I just wanted to take a minute and check in.

As you have probably heard, we just completed our first four-week work cycle. The workload for students comes in waves with every third or fourth week being the time when much graded material is due. It appears like everyone rode the wave successfully, some even surfed it. If I have had concerns, I have been in contact with you individually. My focus is more on process than on results — good process will assure good results.

I continue to check in regularly with the group.

I hope that you are able join us here on campus for Parents' Weekend. If you would like to meet with me, it would be best to set up a time as the weekend is a very busy one. (Note to advisers: before offering this, check with the school calendar, as some institutions actively discourage meetings on particular special weekends).

I look forward to hearing from you.

Note on midterm grades:

Hello Families—

Midterm grades are out and I have shared them with each of my advisees. Your son or daughter should be calling or emailing you soon with those grades. If you don't hear from your student by the end of the day on Friday, please call or email me, and I'll get on the case.

By way of introduction for new families, and review for returning ones, midterm grades are not permanent and shouldn't be viewed as such. They are meant to be a barometer for both students and families to gain a better sense of your child's academic progress and direction. I understand that it may be difficult for many of you to be a great distance away from your teenager and not be able to directly manage his/her academic achievement. Parents of new students especially should know that an academic adjustment period is natural. Over time, with a deliberate and sustained approach to one's studies, the results will usually reflect this effort.

When we next meet, I plan on leading my advisees through the following exercise [cut and paste the exercise you choose here]:

Note about the end of the Fall term:

Hello Families—

I hope that everyone had a great Thanksgiving holiday and that you are gearing up for a long winter break—whether action-packed or relaxing. We celebrate Christmas in the Morrissey household, and with three young kids it is a very festive (hectic) and fun time of year.

The end of the term is rapidly approaching and I wanted to let you know how you can help your children as they prepare for finals. The school's finals are not cumulative, but they are challenging and fall within three or four days, so it is an intense period for the students (and the faculty!).

In my advisee meeting today, I asked students to clean their rooms this weekend and to prepare a good study space for themselves. I hope that they have started that task. I suggested they go through their desks; find their old notes, tests, quizzes, and study guides from the term; and get them in order so that they can use their time most efficiently. Many of our faculty use the school website to store notes and study guides. I reminded students to go to those sites and to bookmark or print the documents they think will be helpful to them. I also told them to ask each of their individual teachers whether there were going to be any extra help sessions in the upcoming weeks.

I gave students a calendar with the daily schedule, the test week schedule, and evening study session times listed on it and encouraged them to think specifically about when and how they would prepare for exams.

Experience has shown that being intentional and deliberate about one's approach to large assignments and tests leads to the best outcomes.

Also, bear in mind that your teen may do nothing but eat and sleep for a few days after school ends. We hear that often from lots and lots of parents. It's completely OK and healthy to give the kids the down time they need. However, it is equally important that a few nights before they return to school kids resume their "school" sleeping schedule. We do our best to encourage them to get to bed between 11 and 11:30 p.m. and most students need to be up and in class by 8 a.m. It helps with re-entry if they follow this pattern for a few nights before returning to campus.

Whether you celebrate Kwanza, Solstice, Christmas, Hanukah, December 25th, or something else in your family, I wish you all a very Happy Holiday season and a joyous New Year. Here's to safe travels for all of our students coming and going from campus.

Thank you for sharing your sons and daughters with us.

Note about the beginning of Spring term:

Hello Families—

Happy New Year!

Spring Term has begun, and for those of you who are new, the term is a long one with work running in three- and four-week cycles of papers and written, graded assignments.

You may hear from your sons and daughters that they are already feeling the effects of winter: encourage them, like I do, to get out into the sunshine (or gray clouds) every day; to exercise daily, and to manage their time carefully. Remember, sleep is crucial to health and well-being!

This week in adviser meeting we reviewed goals from the Fall term and wrote out new ones for this term. Included with the goals were specific individual strategies that students will use to achieve their goals. Ask your child about his/her goals sometime; in this department there's no such thing as too many helpers.

Just as a reminder, my contact numbers are: (h) _____ and (o) _____ and (c) _____. Don't hesitate to call or write with any questions or concerns. Until next time!

Note about course selection and graduation requirements:

Hello Families —

I recently sent your child the following email:

The time to complete your schedule for the upcoming academic year is quickly approaching. Prior to course registration, please carefully read and complete the steps below. (Warning: list is long!)

Scheduling is done electronically on _____. These dates are firm and the deadlines are set in stone; they are deadlines! There will be a slew of emails coming from the Dean's office over the next two weeks; it is crucial that you check your email frequently and carefully read the contents of the messages. There will also be some firm deadlines coming up in the next few weeks and if students miss them, it is very difficult to give them their desired schedule or to make any changes.

Several of the elective courses are limited section courses that are filled by lottery. There will be several forthcoming emails about which courses those are (mostly senior electives and senior studies courses) and how to enter the lottery for those courses. The dates and times that the lottery is open, runs, and then closes are firm; be sure to be aware of these deadlines and act accordingly if you are interested in a course being filled by lottery.

To Do List:

Ask yourself: *What do I need to take to fulfill my graduation requirements?*

Graduation requirements are listed in the Student Handbook.

Start with graduation requirements and build your schedule from there, adding challenge or specific courses that intrigue you afterward. *(As if you need to be reminded at this point in your career, the ethos, expectation, and culture of school is that students take the most challenging selection of courses as they are able and seek as many different instructors as possible.)*

Speak with your current teachers about your placement in the next course in the departmental sequence.

This step takes time—start early! Make an appointment to see your current instructors; tell them why you are requesting a meeting. This gives them time to ponder the variety of courses within their department that might suit you. Your current instructor is the best resource for you to determine which level course and which sequence of courses you should enter for next year. He or she may encourage you to branch out in an interest area (i.e. Probability and Statistics, instead of the second term of Calculus). He or she may encourage you to enter a whole new field within a department (from History to Economics, for example).

We hire very few inexperienced teachers and they are content area experts. It would be wise to listen to their encouragement and advice and to heed it!

Speak with current seniors whom you trust and whom you know have excelled at school:

This is a dangerous, but necessary, step…you will be getting the seniors' opinions, perspectives, outlooks, beliefs, and judgments. Thank them kindly for their input, but consider it within the context that it was given.

11th graders should speak with their college counselor.

This step takes time—start early! Remember that when you go to a college counselor, he or she will advise you on what, in his/her vast experience, is the best course of study. Also remember, that if you decide to take his or her advice, it does not mean that you will get into the college of your choice, and conversely, if you decide against his or her advice, that you have limited your chances at that college. Colleges look at a wide range of factors when deciding on acceptance—seeking leadership positions inside and outside of the school, being involved in extra-curricular activities, and having a sparkling discipline and attendance record are as important to a college as whether you took, to use an example, ENG 320 or 321.

Any student wishing to play a varsity sport at the college level—D 1, 2, or 3 should meet with a college counselor, as the NCAA has course requirements that may affect your course choices.

- Sketch out your courses, in pencil, on paper, and include a second choice for every elective you have chosen.

  Did you really think that I wasn't going to make you write something?

- Talk with your parents about your plan—be prepared to explain why you have chosen one course instead of another or one sequence of courses instead of another.

- Bring the sketch to me.

- Enter the courses online when prompted to do so on April ____.

You will be able to change some courses, but please understand that changing one course may alter your entire schedule and bump you from another choice. *DO NOT change courses without first talking to your parents and to me!* (Be prepared to hear that I do not think the change is advisable....)

Block out a few moments each day over the course of the next few weeks to review the materials and to talk with the people I have suggested. You should have a sketch of courses by April ____ so that we can talk about it and make any changes.

As always, don't hesitate to contact me or to stop by my house or office with questions.

Note about the college process and end of the winter/beginning of springtime:

Hello Families —

This is my "end of winter/beginning of spring" letter that I send out to the parents of my 11th grade advisees around this time every year. I remember first sending it out by mail in 1990; it consisted of eight words: "The college process is beginning for your kid." It gets longer every year.

In this note I try to address and demystify that intergalactic Black Hole otherwise known as the college application and admission process.

College Applications

The college process is very stressful for students, parents, and advisers alike. After more than 20 years, I am chagrinned to admit that the whole adventure remains somewhat of a mystery to me. All we can control is what we can control. In my opinion, that is helping advisees achieve their academic and extracurricular goals, helping them thoroughly research colleges in which they are interested, and having them present themselves as best they can on the application. To this end, I share with you the following thoughts.

Parents should expect a wide range of responses from their sons and daughters as they embark on the college process. Some students lock up and are frozen by fear and the stress that surrounds the process, while others become fanatic researchers as they work furiously to compile a list of colleges. Most teens display a range of emotions and responses—I'm simply advising parents to be ready for a range.

In choosing schools, some students really surprise me; students who are usually methodical and scientific in their approach sometimes choose to apply to colleges based on their emotions. Similarly, other students, who usually appear to be guided purely by feelings, look at statistics and hard data when compiling their list.

Students will need to do some work for the school's College Counseling Office over the summer. This won't win any popularity points with any teenager, but my experience is that students who have done that work over the summer make much more informed college choices than their peers who did not complete the work. Just as a reminder, the college process is very, very, very deadline-oriented, and there is no wiggle room in these deadlines.

Amidst an ocean of uncertainty, one thing that I can say for sure is that the list of colleges that your child will finally choose to apply to will morph, change, and be rearranged many, many, many times over the course of the next six to eight months. Sometimes these changes will make perfect sense to everyone, and sometimes they will only make sense to the student.

Spring Break of the 11th grade year is a great time to begin the college hunting process. The following are suggestions that have worked well for families over the years:

- Take a tour of a local college or university. Simply taking a tour helps students know better what to expect—where the tour guide will direct you, what the other prospective students are wearing, what kinds of questions other prospective students are asking. If you live in an area where it is possible, it might be helpful to tour a state school and a private school to see if there is a different feel to each one.

- *Before* creating a list of colleges, break the country into four quadrants—Northeast, Southeast, Northwest, and Southwest and help your student consider the pros and cons of attending a college in each area. (If your child has expressed an interest in applying to schools overseas or in Canada, do this for those parts of the globe as well.) Discuss the pros and cons of attending a large (usually, but not always, public) college vs. the pros and cons of attending a small (usually, but not always, private) college. Discuss the pros and cons of attending a traditional college vs. a non-traditional one. For the Northeast, a traditional college might be Boston College, and an example of a non-traditional college might be the College of the Atlantic. Finally, research schools that offer programs specific to your child's interests. After completing this exercise, a potential list of colleges to research further should begin to emerge.

- Prepare your student and yourselves to work with the school's College Counseling Office (CCO). The philosophy of the CCO is that this process should be very student-driven; it is, after all, the student who will attend college. The CCO and the college process in general are very deadline-oriented; make sure that your son or daughter understands the importance of meeting the deadlines. Another guiding philosophy of the CCO is that each student, come this time next year, has more than one college choice. Understand that CCO staffers will push your child to finalize a list of applications that has a wide range. That is sometimes difficult and frustrating for some students to understand when they walk into their first meeting with their counselor and have Harvard, Princeton, Stanford, and Oxford as their safety schools.

Thanks for reading. As always, don't hesitate to contact me with questions. Enjoy your time with your children over Spring Break!

Further Reading/Resources

A Mind at a Time. Levine, M. New York: Simon and Schuster, 2003.

Achieving and Sustaining Institutional Excellence. Barefoot, *et al.* San Francisco: Jossey-Bass, 2005.

The Blessing of a B Minus. W. Mogel. New York: Scribner, 2011.

Bowling Alone. Putnam, R. New York: Simon and Schuster, 2000.

Building a Residential Curriculum. Hotchkiss and Kowalchick. Durango: Durango Institute Press, 2002.

Character and Coaching: Building Virtue in Athletic Programs. Yeager *et al.* Port Chester: Dude Publishing, 2001.

Educating for Character: How our Schools Can Teach Respect and Responsibility. Lickona, T. New York: Bantam, 1991.

Family Matters: How Schools Can Cope With the Crisis in Child-Rearing. Evans, R. San Francisco: Jossey Bass, 2004.

Far and Wide: Diversity in the American Boarding School. Edited by Hillman and Thorn. Gilsum: Avocus Publishing, 1997.

First Year Advising, A Compendium of Best Practices. Edited by Tardy. Notre Dame: University of Notre Dame Press, 2009.

Generation MySpace: Helping Your Teen Survive Online Adolescence. Kelsey, C. New York: Marlowe & Co., 2007

Healthy Choices, Healthy Schools. Edited by Crosier. Gilsum: Avocus Publishing, 1992.

Highly Effective Programs: Character Education in Independent Schools. The CSEE Moral Development Team. Portland, OR.: Council for Spiritual and Ethical Education, 2007.

The Intentional Teacher. Gow, P. Gilsum: Avocus Publishing, 2009.

Odd Girl Out: The Hidden Culture of Aggression in Girls. R. Simmons. New York: Mariner Books, 2003.

Promoting Social and Emotional Learning. Elias, *et al.* Alexandria: Association for Supervision & Curriculum Development, 1997.

Punished by Rewards: The Trouble with Gold Stars, Incentive Plans, A's, Praise, and Other Bribes. Kohn, A. Boston: Houghton Mifflin, 1999.

Quests and Quandaries. Hotchkiss, C. Gilsum: Avocus Publishing, 2001.

Ready to Use Social Skills Lessons & Activities. Begun, R. San Francisco: Jossey Bass, 1996.

The Big Book of Team Building Games. Newstrom and Scannell. New York: McGraw-Hill, 1998.

The Essential Guide to Talking with Gifted Teens: Ready-to-Use Discussions About Identity, Stress, Relationships, and More. Peterson, J. Minneapolis: Free Spirit, 2008.

The Frailty Myth: Redefining the Physical Potential of Women and Girls. Dowling, C. New York: Random House, 2001.

The Optimistic Child. Seligman, M. Boston: Houghton Mifflin, 1995.

The Pressured Child. Thompson, M. New York: Ballantine Books, 2004.

The Primal Teen: What the New Discoveries About the Teenage Brain Tell Us About Our Kids. Strauch, B. New York, Anchor Books, 2004.

The Summer Camp Handbook. Thurber and Malinowski. Glendale: Perspective, 2002.

Understanding by Design. Wiggins and McTighe. Upper Saddle River: Merrill/Prentice Hall, 2005.

Unhooked: How Young Women Pursue Sex, Delay Love and Lose at Both. Stepp, L. New York: Riverhead Trade, 2008.

What Smart Students Know: Maximum Grades. Optimum Learning. Minimum Time. Robinson, A. New York: Three Rivers Press, 1993.

Words That Wound. Matsuda *et al.* Boulder: Westview Press, 1993.

Yes, Your Teen is Crazy!: Loving Your Kid Without Losing Your Mind. M. Bradley. Gig Harbor: Harbor Press, 2002.

Your College Experience. Garner, *et al.* Boston: Thomas Wadsworth, 2007.

Dan Morrissey has 20 years of teaching, advising, and administrative experience in independent schools. He is currently Dean of Students at Phillips Exeter Academy, in Exeter, N.H., and has extensive national experience in the areas of student affairs and support. A tireless advocate and presenter on student health, wellness, and safety, Morrissey is a faculty member of The Association of Boarding Schools (TABS) Summer Institute, as well as the Durango Institute for Co-Curricular Education. He comes from a family of dedicated educators, and lives in Exeter with his three children. He enjoys surfing, wet kisses from puppies, and lately, blogging on his favorite subject at www.theadvisersblog.com.